ADVANCE PRAISE

"*Building an Uncommon Champion* offers great insights to parents and coaches who want to build better athletes, and more importantly who want to help kids become leaders, with the integrity, compassion and courage to make this world a better place."

–DAN BRULÉ, author of
Just Breathe: Mastering Breathwork.

"Jennifer's new book, *Building an Uncommon Champion*, is a must read! She educates and inspires the reader on steps to achieve self-mastery, leadership, and most importantly, how to bring glory to God with the gifts they have been given!"

–GREG AMUNDSON, #1 bestselling author of
The Warrior and The Monk

"Being exceptional is not easy - let Jennifer Matras show you the way. I recommend this book to all those interested in being their best selves."

–MICHAEL MASSUCCI, author of
An Elite Journey: A Young Man's Leadership Story

T0150765

Building an Uncommon Champion

BUILDING AN UNCOMMON CHAMPION

Help Your Child Redefine Success

JENNIFER MATRAS

NEW YORK

LONDON • NASHVILLE • MELBOURNE • VANCOUVER

BUILDING AN UNCOMMON CHAMPION

Help Your Child Redefine Success

Published in New York, New York, by Morgan James Publishing. Morgan James is a trademark of Morgan James, LLC. www.MorganJamesPublishing.com

ISBN 9781642793543 paperback
ISBN 9781642793550 eBook
ISBN 9781642793567 audio
Library of Congress Control Number: 2018913363

Cover Design by:
Christopher Kirk
www.GFSstudio.com

Interior Design by:
Chris Treccani
www.3dogcreative.net

Morgan James is a proud partner of Habitat for Humanity Peninsula and Greater Williamsburg. Partners in building since 2006.

Get involved today! Visit
MorganJamesPublishing.com/giving-back

To my Lord and Savior Jesus Christ who has given me the unconditional love that's deeply desired in all our hearts.

TABLE OF CONTENTS

FOREWORD

During my early adult life, I made the first good decision of my life… to stop listening to others and to follow my heart. This led me to the Navy SEALs, where I dedicated myself to becoming the best. As a SEAL and now trainer of SEALs, I made sure to search for mentors, learn from the experts, follow tried and true warrior traditions and strive to master myself daily so I could serve more powerfully. My motto became "one day, one life" expressing the warrior code of taking things one day at a time, keeping things simple, and always learning and growing.

I have really enjoyed meeting others who love to learn and strive for mastery through my training programs of SEALFIT and Unbeatable Mind. Jennifer Matras is one of those people. She is completely dedicated to becoming the best leader in her domain, the type of individual committed to warrior virtues that this world desperately needs. And she is passionate about sharing her knowledge and skills to help others.

Jennifer Matras is more than a skating expert and strength coach. She is also a spiritual mentor to thousands seeking to better themselves through their sport. Jennifer helps them maximize performance, improve strength, and improve over-all health. Yet, what makes her special is that she knows performance and winning is not the most important… that the physical realm is but one domain to master. We must also master the mental, emotional and spiritual domains as well.

Jennifer uses her expertise to help others become their best and leverages the experiences from Unbeatable Mind and the arduous SEALFIT crucible training called the "20X" into her training programs. She understands that the unique and powerful values of the Navy SEALs, and other elite warrior traditions, can help modern warrior-athletes tap into their "kokoro spirits", work together as authentic teammates, and transcend the limiting attitude of winning at the expense of others. She fosters a culture of accountability, humility and selflessness, and in turn helps her trainees find satisfaction in overcoming hard challenges. Understanding the power of one's mind and emotional resiliency, she uses these tools to help others learn we are always 20X more capable than we think we are.

It takes passion and perseverance to work towards one's goals, and Jennifer's decades of research and practice allow her to create breakthrough results. This book, *Building an Uncommon Champion*, will provide great insight on these principles, and if you take her seriously, and do the work, you too will build the life and success you have dreamed. Hooyah!

Mark Divine
Founder, SEALFIT, Inc., Unbeatable, LLC
Best selling author: *The Way of the SEAL* and *Unbeatable Mind*

You Were Born for a Purpose

"I praise you because I am fearfully and wonderfully made;
Your works are wonderful, I know that full well."
-PSALM 119:14

Did you know that God doesn't make mistakes? What an amazing gift of hope scripture gives us, that "God works all things out for good of those who love him, who have been called according to his purpose." Your child was born for a purpose – an amazing, unique purpose brought into this world, at this time in history, with a certain personality and gifts only they can utilize. They have amazing abilities and a love driven by the universe that can only be lived out in this world through them. If they don't use these abilities and gifts, then it will be like a part of God dies within them.

All too often people allow fear, doubt, and laziness to take ahold of their lives and keep them from being all the things God knows they can become. Unfortunately, we have a brain that can cause us to go to the negative end of the spectrum. They keep us in our comfort zone, away from danger and struggles. This prevents us from doing the things we need to do to become better and reach our potential. Your child has dreams, big dreams – yet why do some people reach their goals and others don't? Why do some people run wholeheartedly toward their dreams regardless of the obstacles, while others hit the snooze button and stay in bed where things are comfortable?

Your child was born to be a champion, but let's build an *uncommon* champion. There are plenty of coaches out there who improve skills, build strengths, and get weaknesses to diminish in their athletes, but to be an uncommon champion it's about so much more.

Are you ready to learn about the principles which will help your child not only reach their dreams, but also give them life-long tools to sustain their success? Are you ready to learn about techniques that will build your child's emotional resiliency, commitment, and leadership skills which are proven to get results? Let's leave common for someone else and grow in the journey that God has us on to be all that we can possibly be. If you are ready, let's go!

CHAPTER 1:

So, Your Kid Wants to Make It to the NHL, Huh?

"What you become directly influences what you get."
-JIM ROHN, 12 PILLARS

I've had the blessing of working with thousands of different hockey players. Anywhere from beginners who couldn't do hockey stops, all the way up to the professional level that showed remarkable speed and power. I've had amazing students over the years who wouldn't leave a lesson without making sure to thank me for my time. Then I've had higher level players who acted like two-year-olds if they couldn't do a certain drill I demonstrated. I've seen players who I thought would make it to the NHL end up only in the beer leagues. Then there have been others I thought were going to break their ankles in some of my skating drills end up making millions of dollars playing the sport they love. Why is it that some make it to the highest level, but most others don't?

There are reasons people come up with to explain why people end up where they do. It could be one's circumstances – such as their home life – or it's God's ultimate plan, or one was born with more "talent" than another. I agree with these statements. But, did you know that no one can locate a "talent gene"? I find that fascinating.

We are all born with more potential than we realize! Why is it that there are some people who are born handicapped make it to the major leagues, play professional golf, or even surf some insane waves? Helen Keller was blind and deaf but has been an inspiration to millions. There are many stories of professional athletes who were born into a less-than-ideal family situation who have shown a stellar work ethic, unbelievable discipline, and daily commitment to their goals. We can think of several examples of people who defy the odds, prove others wrong, and go on to win championships.

Remember, your child was born with unique gifts and abilities. So, how do we make sure we give them all the opportunities to keep them on the path to success? How can we make sure to prevent bad habits, keep them away from injuries and keep them from experiencing burnout? There are many factors that tie into building a champion, especially an uncommon champion. Many people will say the odds are stacked against your child making it to their goals, and the numbers would suggest they're right. On average, there are 1.5 million people in the world playing hockey. Every single one of the players I have worked with has said they wanted to get to the NHL.

Just like them, your child is competing against the other million players to get there. With only 31 teams in the NHL, that means there are only 620 spots available to play on an NHL team. Some players may have goals of just getting to play college hockey. Again, with at least a million players working to get even a college scholarship there are only 60 Division 1 teams, which leaves only 1,200 spots available. And that number is even smaller at any given time!

Playing college hockey is a great accomplishment. It can lead to the ultimate goal of the NHL. But how does one get there? One should question if there are common traits shown amongst these athletes who do make it to play at these high levels. I believe there are common denominators amongst the elite, but it's more than just what month your child may be born in, what height and weight they are or how many hours they practice shooting and working at their skills.

There is Always a Chance

The chance is small of making it to the highest level in anything. But I focus on the fact that there is a chance! There are steps or principles that can give someone a better chance of reaching their goals, but shouldn't the ultimate focus be more about how one is growing as a human being? It's exciting to continue to grow in one's skills, but should we follow others who do it at the expense of hurting other human beings? Should we just focus on greed and status?

I say, "Absolutely not!" Working to become part of that one percent who get to the professional level takes thousands of hours, commitment, and many people or coaches to improve skills, strength and speed, to name a few things. Ultimately, what I love to focus on is not just one's outer appearance but one's heart. Scripture says, "for man looks at the outward appearance, but the Lord looks at the heart" (1 Samuel 16:7). Let's see how important one's heart is to become uncommon.

You Can't Measure Heart

The stress and anxiety that come along with yearly hockey tryouts never cease to amaze me. It's good to have to work to be part of a team. Young kids need to undergo the disappointment of not making a team or having to make new friends when joining a new environment. But what can really frustrate me is when a kid comes to me and says the reason a coach didn't take them is because of their size.

"They said I was too small," they say.

"Too small?" I ask. "Have they seen the size of your heart?"

Height and weight are just numbers. Though many coaches seem to think they need big players, especially defensemen, if a player doesn't have heart, I don't care what size they are. I have worked with so many players who were big at the younger age compared to their peers and it only hurt them in the long run. They are picked to be on teams for their size which causes them to gain bad habits, horrible work ethic, poor skating mechanics and less than ideal character.

The focus on size for kids at a younger age is truly a detriment. I've had so many players who get to the higher levels where most kids end up being the same height and weight. Now these kids who have been "big" their whole lives get passed up for the kids who have had better work ethic for years.

You can't measure heart! Usually the kids who have been the smaller ones at the younger age not only understand work ethic, leadership, and commitment, but they also have mental toughness. They understand adversity and how to deal with it on a personal level without it breaking them. It's beautiful to see and so enjoyable to coach. I like to tell parents, "If you love your child, you will let them struggle."

If your kid wants to make it to the NHL, then get them into situations where they have to embrace challenges, overcome obstacles, and face adversity. It's tough to watch a kid struggle, and sometimes we wish the adversity wouldn't have to happen, but adversity is the catalyst to growth. These are the traits that will lead one to success. It will give them the character to work toward their goals and to help them on the journey to the NHL, and more importantly in life.

With the numbers being slim of making it to the NHL, I never focus on them. Many coaches or parents will say, "They're never going to make it to the pros." I don't think about this. No one has a crystal ball. No one can see the future. I believe whenever I am working with athletes they can be the next "Great One." Why not? If you don't believe you can get somewhere, then you're already placing a negative thought out into the universe. We win first in the mind. So, visualize the best outcomes and believe that getting to the NHL is possible! It does take work, and a lot of uncommon work. But if one loves what they are doing, then it is actually fun. Too many of my students will look at training sessions or challenges as being "hard." I say to them, "Is that a bad thing?"

Retired Navy SEAL and author Mark Divine, says, "Destroy the myth that easy is good and hard is bad." I love that. If one wants to grow then they have to do what is hard, but it is actually a good thing! Because most likely you are growing! Frederick Douglass, who was a social reformer and abolitionist, said, "If there is no struggle, there is no progress." Therefore, the road to the NHL is not easy; otherwise everyone would make it to the professional level.

Those who reach their goals are uncommon, and it is uncommon behaviors, thoughts, and emotions that get one there. Things in life that come easy aren't worthwhile. The elite athletes know this. The great ones know their weaknesses and work on those instead of doing what comes easy to them. They have the heart to keep working, the mental toughness to embrace adversity and the humility to know they can always keep getting better. This is the beginning of the uncommon road to building an uncommon champion.

Reflection Questions

Questions for athletes:

1. Can you think of a time when you faced adversity and enjoyed it, knowing it would make you grow?

2. Where have you shown the most heart toward something, especially if someone rejected you or told you that you couldn't accomplish something?

3. How do you feel about something that comes hard to you versus easy?

4. Do you have goals? Are they written down on paper?

Questions for parents:

1. How do you feel when you see your child face adversity?

2. Do you feel you allow your child to take the easier road versus the harder path that will make them grow?

3. How do you hold your child accountable with the goals they have written down but without harping on them?

CHAPTER 2:

Facing the Truth

*"There is nothing enlightened about shrinking
so that other people won't feel insecure around you."*
-**Marianne Williamson, Our Deepest Fear**

I never thought I would put on skates or step foot inside an ice arena for the rest of my life. My figure skating career was done after fourteen long years. Though I felt kind of relieved, I also felt lost. Figure skating was the one thing that was a constant in my life since I was three-and-a-half years old. My parents put my older sister and myself into figure skating when we were very young, and it became our life as a family. We missed holidays with relatives, left school early daily to get to the rink for training, and missed weeks of school throughout the year for competitions. We were optimistic as competitive figure skaters. Our parents did whatever they could to make ends meet and see to it that we had the best coaching possible to help us work toward our dreams.

Sports can teach us a lot. They can teach us about commitment, focus, discipline, responsibility, and the importance of consistent work ethic. However, I wish when I was younger that someone would have taught me about the power of one's attitude. Did you know the two things we can control in life are our attitudes and our work ethic? In figure skating, it's easy to learn early on that work ethic is important. You have limited time to learn how to jump higher, spin faster, and keep learning new maneuvers. If you don't improve, you don't win competitions. You don't move on to higher levels. Pretty simple concept, but no one taught me about the power of attitude. Let me tell you, I had a sour one that began early on and seemed to progress as I got older.

Sometimes my attitude would give me a chip on my shoulder and really help me focus on improving which led to some success in my career. Around age 11, my parents found a coach who I connected with and who seemed to care about me more than just being a competitive machine. I began to win competitions with him, which led to moving up to higher levels, but also led to more pressure and demands to keep improving. Under this coach's guidance, I began to win some big local competitions, and received championship titles at my age. My sister was also winning major competitions, and even getting national recognition. Though all of this was exciting and made all the training seem worth it, it also led to more pressures at home, and even a move to a different skating club where better coaching was available and national and Olympic athletes were also training.

The Pain of Discipline versus the Pain of Regret

One would think the culture of being around higher-level athletes would be exciting and motivating to keep pushing one's self. It did for my sister. Unfortunately for me, I found myself at odds with the environment. There would be moments of great success and the feeling of being on top of the world, and then the next week I would lose all joy and drive of wanting to get better. I found myself distracted with the pressures of high school, and I wanted to experience what my peers were.

Our life as a family revolved around figure skating for most of my childhood, which did teach me many great life skills, but it also kept me from having sleepovers or going to school functions. I really didn't have many friends from school. Once I got to high school, there was a part of me that didn't want to be left out anymore, regardless of how it may hurt my skating career. This, of course, led to a quick regression of my skating performance in practice, and an even more embarrassing showing at competitions.

As my sister was continuing to perform at high levels, I continued to go down the wrong path with the wrong crowd in high school. It didn't take long for increasingly bad choices to be taken, which led to the final week of skating for me. My sister and mother were out of town at the national competition one weekend, and I decided to lie to my father and go to a party with friends. As one can imagine, this didn't end well.

I was succumbing to peer pressure and began drinking heavily with a group of friends at a campfire. Another life lesson that I wish someone would have taught me – we are the average of the five people we hang around with most. If I had dreams of becoming an Olympian, it would be pretty hard to accomplish when I was hanging out with alcoholic teenagers. While at this party my father called my friend's parents and learned that I had lied about my whereabouts. My friend's mother called us and said I had to get home immediately, and that the state police were out looking for me. I'm not sure to this day if that was something my dad made up, but I somehow got home without hurting anyone. It's something I still wish I hadn't done, and I believe God kept me and others safe on the road that night.

Once my father knew I lied and had come home drunk, it was the end of my figure skating career. There was an obvious lack of discipline. I felt the pain of regret.

Did you know there are two different pains in life? There is the pain of discipline and the pain of regret. Discipline is the bridge that connects one's goals to results. Not sure why I thought drinking with friends was going to give me the results I hoped for in my skating career. It's so important for one to learn about the power of discipline. Though it may feel painful in the moment, it is nothing compared having the pain of regret due to poor choices.

I was a senior in high school, and had never known life without skating. I sat and stared at the clock. I felt empty, because it was the same time that I had left school early for the previous decade of my life. It would be the first time I would be leaving school just like the rest of the students, instead of being privileged to be gone an hour early for training.

Though I was angry with my parents for making me quit skating, I knew it was for the best. They had sacrificed so much to get my sister and me to such high levels. I felt like I failed them. However, skating would take me to a whole other direction that I never would have guessed.

God Has a Plan

In the book of Proverbs, scripture says that we may plan our way, but the Lord ultimately directs our steps. It's as if when we make plans, God tilts his head with a smirk and says, "Really?" When my skating career was done, I didn't think I would ever step into an arena again. But God clearly wanted something different.

I had just arrived home from school one day and the house phone rang. It was my sister. She was calling from the arena and she was in a panic.

"Get your skates! I need your help!" she said.

"What? I don't understand," I said.

"We are starting learn-to-skate classes today, and one of the instructors didn't show up. Can you please get here as soon as you can?" she begged.

To my surprise, I remembered where my skates were at and arrived at the arena just in time to help with the lessons. Without even going over instructions or taking any time to prepare, I was suddenly thrown into a coaching position. I was working with little kids who were crying, frightened, and being handed over to me by their moms and dads.

I began to sing songs, take them on imaginary plane rides or trips to the ice cream store. This got the kids to follow me around the ice, squat down, jump up to practice balance and coordination, all the while beginning to build a trust with me. The experience melted my hardened heart, and I fell in love with being inside an ice rink again. The unbelievable joy of helping kids learn how to skate could not be put into words.

One Female Versus Many Hockey Boys

As I continued as a very enthusiastic skating instructor with the kids, a hockey coach put in a request to have one of us help with his power skating class he was about to offer. I immediately jumped at the opportunity. As competitive figure skaters, we had power skating sessions throughout our training to help build power, work capacity, and to work on additional mechanics. I didn't want to pass this up to help others.

On my first day, I couldn't believe how nervous I was. I was on the ice with a bunch of males in hockey pads, and I was just a senior in high school with my figure skates on thinking I could tell a group of boys what to do. I decided to follow the head coach's lead, but he could see how nervous I was. He forced me to speak in front of the group.

"Lead the next drill, Jennifer," he commanded.

I must have looked like a deer in headlights. I remember the drill to this day. It was a simple drill of teaching the kids to put their knees down on the ice. It's sometimes referred to as "Russian knees." I was nervous, but it was exactly what I needed – to be pushed outside my comfort zone. Philosopher Neale Donald Walsch has an amazing quote that says, "Life begins at the end of your comfort zone." I learned at the age of eighteen how true that statement is and have continued to live by it throughout my life.

If someone would have told me on that magical day of coaching that I would go on to work with high school teams, college players, and would even help players get to the NHL, I would have laughed and thought the person was on drugs. But, again, when God has a plan, He has a plan that must be fulfilled.

Over the first couple of years, I would teach skating lessons at 6 a.m. at a local ice rink before school, while also going to school for a veterinary technician degree. I would work at a local veterinary hospital, go to school and also teach skating whenever I could find time. When I was around twenty years old, I met a very successful business owner who told me to figure out what I love to do in life and then figure out how to make money doing it. I always kept that statement in the back of my mind as I continued to work at a veterinary hospital and teach hockey players on the side. It was a great life lesson, because he never said to chase money. He told me to figure out what I love to do!

As a few more years passed, my coaching demands for helping hockey players continued to keep growing. I was getting more hockey teams requesting my services, my individual lessons continued to stay consistent, and I was also being told to charge more money due to the results I was producing. Seeing players continue to improve brought me joy which was opposite of how I felt driving home from dealing with arrogant veterinary doctors, getting bitten by cats, or seeing dogs neglected or abused. I knew what I had to do. The risk I had to take was scary, but again, those who have the most courage in life take the most risks. I put in my two-week notice with the veterinary hospital and never looked back.

I was on full-force to continue helping hockey players overcome their skating deficiencies. It was amazing to focus on helping others reach their dreams. I was able to use the fourteen years of figure skating and pass it on to help others find more joy, confidence, and rewards in their sport. This led me to realize that I didn't just want to help hockey players become better skaters, I also wanted to help them become better overall athletes. I began to search online what the best degree was to help build better athletes. A few months later, I was enrolled in the Exercise Science program at Eastern Michigan University. A year after that, I was working with the USA National Development Program and learned from them how to truly build the best hockey players.

Upon graduating from the exercise physiology program, I began to train the players I was skating with to do squats, Olympic lifts, and how to reduce the risk of injury. Unfortunately, it was not an easy sell. Not too many men want to learn how to get stronger from a girl. I had already learned how to face adversity and persevere, and to show others what I am capable of from years of figure skating. Being a female in a male dominated sport on top of wanting to help them get stronger in the weight room has definitely been a journey of battling EGOs, arrogance, and entitlement. Luckily, God has given me an attitude where I respond by saying, "Bring it on."

I absolutely loved the training I was doing with players in the weight room. Again, I had found even more of a passion to help others learn and grow. I began to understand the importance of mindset, embracing challenges and recognizing how many people let fear control their life. Instead of getting frustrated or wanting to quit, I trained harder. I even asked the owner of an ice rink if I could revamp the run-down weight room and take it over. He was all for it. Taking this space over led me to meeting one of the local high school team's head coaches. He was not happy about the new rules of the weight room, let alone a female being in charge. After a phone conversation explaining my education, experience with the USA National program, and my understanding of skating mechanics, I boldly told him I could help his team get stronger, improve their performance and peak in playoffs leading them to a possible run for a state championship. Something the program had never accomplished.

It was not easy to get the players or the parents on board with the training, but the head coach was sold on what I could bring to the team. That year the team won every game apart from one tie and went on to win the program's very first state championship. It was one of the top ten moments of my life. There is a quote by a French writer, Moliere, which states, "The greater the obstacle, the more glory in overcoming it." With so much to prove in my first year of training a team with strength and conditioning, and the amount of push back I got from the players made the state championship that much more glorious.

Things started to go to a new level at this point. I began to work with more high-level players and more teams wanted to train both on and off the ice with me. I was constantly working, running from the ice to the weight room and back to the ice. Yet, like the mentor told me earlier in my life, it felt like I was hardly working because of the amount of joy I was getting from seeing so many athletes improve.

One was a college player – I'll call him Jason – who came to me for some much-needed skating lessons. He and I would have some transformational years ahead of us which would lead to a better understanding of what the beginning of building an uncommon champion looks like. Things like focus, discipline, and work ethic to always want to become better. And it has to be done consistently at uncommon levels. If one wants to be better than others, they can't be doing what the rest of the common crowd is doing. And these are a few things of what got Jason to the NHL.

REFLECTION QUESTIONS

Questions for athletes:

1. How do you feel about missing out on things with friends or family due to training and working at being uncommon?

2. What are the two things we can control in life?

3. What are the two different pains in life?

4. Have you ever felt regret and how did you learn from it?

5. In what area in your life do you need to become more disciplined to get the results you want?

6. When have you been pushed outside your comfort zone which ultimately helped you grow?

7. What are you doing that is more than what your peers are doing to be uncommon?

Questions for parents:

1. How do you help your kids have balance between staying focused on goals yet still hanging out with friends or going to school functions from time to time?

2. How do you remind your child that they have control over their attitude?

3. How have you helped your child learn from the pain of regret, so they learn to stay more disciplined toward their goals yet not feel like they are missing anything?

4. How are you showing your kids that you enjoy getting outside your comfort zone in life?

CHAPTER 3:

On to the NHL

"You are imperfect. You are wired for struggle,
but you are worthy of love and belonging."
-BRENÉ BROWN, DARING GREATLY

During one summer program, a few college players started coming to see me to help improve their skating skills. It was in this group that Jason showed up to my training sessions. He really seemed to stand out. Yes, all the players were similar in height, weight, and speed, but it was Jason who came to the lessons more often than the others. More importantly, he would be the only one to come early to warm up and stay late to do off-ice training. One day we even had a lesson scheduled for 6 a.m., and when I pulled into the parking lot he was already warming up outside the rink. That was definitely uncommon – no one else had ever beaten me to the rink or onto the ice before lessons!

When I began working with Jason, he had no NHL teams or scouts looking at him. He was a fourth line player and didn't dress consistently with his team. By the time he reached his senior year of playing at the Division 1 level, he began to get looks for his increased speed, agility, and overall performance. It was a great improvement in performance in such a short period of time.

Even though I was producing some great speed with players and improving overall performance in high-level athletes, one day I realized I wanted to do things in addition to just skating and off-ice training. During one week of training, there was some homework I had given to this group of college players regarding psychology. Pretty strange, right? Why not focus more on how strong one can become or do video analysis? Because that isn't what being uncommon is all about. In this certain piece of homework, the questions focused how one feels about their attitude and how much drive or motivation one must improve their performance. Players answered on a scale one to ten, one being the least on the scale and ten being the highest to be able to control a situation. When I got Jason's answers back, he admitted he felt like he had no control over his attitude. He even had the lowest score – a one – next to the question!

I was shocked! I couldn't believe such a highly skilled player on one of the best D1 programs in the country didn't realize he could choose the kind of attitude he had. It was almost like I was talking to my younger self. It was a transformation, I believe, in Jason's life realizing that we can choose how we face each day.

I shared with him what I wish someone would have shared with me when I was younger regarding attitude. Poet Charles Swindoll writes, "I am convinced the longer I live that life is 10 percent of what happens to me and 90 percent how I respond to it." Yes! We can choose how we respond to things that happen to us.

What are your thoughts on this quote? Do you respond with positivity to whatever is thrown your way in life?

One year later, Jason went from playing college to getting picked up by an NHL team. I was so excited for him! During the first season, while playing for their farm team in New York, he got his lucky break. The commitment of coming to the rink early, staying late, and doing thousands of hard laps on the ice finally paid off. He got called up to play in the "show." Though I'm sure he was nervous, he took his newly refined attitude, increased speed, and ability to fly around defensemen and showed the world what he could do. He had made it.

He not only made it, but he landed a contract for over twenty million dollars. He was never called back down to the farm league, but instead went on to have a career so few in the NHL can ever say they've had. He's had several seasons of 40 points or more, and has accomplished something so few have done which is have a career in the NHL for over a decade.

Today, when I ask Jason what he did to separate himself from others, he explains, "When I was fifteen years old, I looked around and knew I had to do more than what my peers were doing in order to go farther than them." This was the beginning of witnessing what becoming an uncommon champion looked like for me due to his focus, consistent work ethic, and ability to handle criticism, but I was also learning the journey is about so much more than just one's physical abilities.

Am I Worthy?

Figure skating is a beautiful sport. It's graceful, powerful, defies the law of gravity, and can bring a group of people together to celebrate the artistry of the skater and their performance. The competition between opponents can bring excitement to those at the top of their career forcing them to bring all they can to the ice to win a gold medal.

During my career, I experienced moments of performing at my best as if it was effortless. I was observing myself outside my body. I also had performances where I was able to engage and have fun with the audience, bringing them into my program and feeling their energy from one element to the next. It was magical.

Yet, just like other athletes, I also had experiences where it looked as if I had never done this sport in my life. In those moments, I felt I embarrassed my parents, my coaches, and myself. There was one competition where my skate kept coming untied, and I wanted to just get off the ice and go hide. There was also another performance where I fell on a jump right in front of the judges and mouthed a few cuss words. Embarrassing, right? Figure skating can make you feel extremely exposed, vulnerable, and as if the whole world is thinking you should quit the sport if you have a poor performance. Even if one has their best day, it is still ultimately up to other human beings to judge whether you are worthy or not of a medal. I even remember a competition where I didn't perform horribly but it also wasn't my best. The judges still somehow awarded me a medal. My mother's reaction was as if it was a joke and that I didn't deserve any positive recognition at all. I remember my heart dropping, feeling full of shame, which led to a big breakdown.

Everywhere I looked, my identity was wrapped up in what others were telling me about who I was as a person and an athlete. Can I ever be worthy or feel acceptance? Was I worthy to even be a figure skater? How much harder was I supposed to work to feel like I belonged here? How many medals or titles did I have to win to feel loved? It wasn't until later in my journey that I realized our identity shouldn't come from awards, titles, or even what other humans think of us. Our identity comes from something so much greater than ourselves.

This is something I often see with hockey players as well on both sides of the spectrum. Kids feel shame if they don't perform well for their coaches, agents, or parents. On the flipside, players will begin to lack humility and act as if they are the greatest thing to this world because everyone is praising them for their skills and their accomplishments regardless of how they treat their teammates or friends. Isn't life about so much more?

Arena to Cathedral

As I continued to work with Jason, he would invite me to come watch his team practices along with enjoy the luxuries of being at the professional level. I began to get increasing recognition as a skating instructor from high-level coaches, other players, and even some Hall of Famers. I had a blast meeting so many people. It was great to watch Jason have so much fun seeing the rewards of what uncommon discipline, focus, and commitment toward improvement can bring. Jason kept putting more and more points up on the scoreboard throughout the years, even resulting in a 5-point game, which is not an easy accomplishment in the peewee leagues, let alone in the NHL. What was really neat to witness was him becoming a fan favorite with his new NHL team, which caused the crowd to chant his last name when he touched the puck to rush up the ice. Can you hear the crowd chant your player's name now if they put the uncommon work in like Jason?

Ironically, even though there was some great success being shown on the ice, I still wasn't fully satisfied with his skating mechanics or performance. My critique of him happened no matter how many points he did or didn't score. What was great about this was he not only welcomed this critical feedback, but he was also giving me things to think about as well. Personal things, which at first I didn't really notice. It was just seeds being planted.

We didn't always get along – like the time he stormed off the ice, slamming his stick frustrated at the drills, or the time I left him in the weight room because of his selfish attitude. But after lessons we would have discussions about Jesus, or he would invite me to go to church. This wasn't just a one-way relationship between a student and teacher, where the student is always being taught. This was also a situation where the student was teaching the teacher. This is a trait of the uncommon. Too often kids are taught to sit down and shut up. Teachers seem to rarely let kids voice their thoughts, talk in small groups, or express their emotions. Sadly, coaches don't seem to be much better. What I love about being uncommon and building uncommon champions is that you get to create a culture where everyone can talk, lead, encourage, hold others accountable, and teach. It's not just about who holds the power of "authority." If it wasn't for Jason having the courage to talk about Jesus, I wouldn't have learned what he had to teach me. I'd still be like the rest of the common crowd.

One night after a hockey game, Jason asked if I would be interested in going to church in the morning.

"Sure," I answered with some hesitation.

I was really taken back in the beginning. The first thing I noticed was that there was no altar. The traditional Catholic churches that I was familiar with had organs and pipes for the music. This church had drums and guitars. There was no cross or crucified Jesus, but instead there was a Pastor who wore jeans and a t-shirt. The casual wardrobe threw me off, but it helped me connect more with the pastor and his message. It was the beginning of learning more about relationships and less about religion.

Unconditional Love

I began to reflect on all my other relationships. They were performance based. Not unconditional but conditional. All my life I performed for love and attention. The awards we focused on were perishable only to become tarnished and forgotten. There was no talk of grace or mercy. And adults were the ones who were always right. I began to realize that life and sports didn't have to be this way!

Think about how kids feel if they are paid money by their parents or grandparents if they score goals. What about just being a good teammate instead? Being paid to perform takes away from the pure enjoyment of the game for kids and is an example of conditional love. What if players are benched at a young age and never get an explanation of why they aren't getting ice time? This puts into the kid's heads that they aren't worthy unless they perform or are the best player on the team. What if they really are giving their absolute best effort though?

Years ago, I had the pleasure of working with the son of a hall-of-fame NHL player. One day I asked him a few questions regarding hockey and how coaching is done in youth sports. Regarding how coaches bench players to get more effort from them he stated, "Benching players at a young age is the easy way out for coaches. The coach is missing the whole point of what it means to be a coach and teach positive life lessons." These situations can be very detrimental to kids. How adults and coaches treat their athletes will result in how the kids view themselves. Especially if the kids don't know about the God that unconditionally loves them regardless of their performance.

When I found out about the love God has for me through His son Jesus Christ, my world changed forever. I made a promise to myself to help kids see there is a much better way to live life and play sports. And it's not to selfishly please another human being. There is a path and a process to becoming the best person and leader one can be and let me tell you, it's not following the rest of our culture! Being an uncommon champion doesn't only refer to being a champion in the arena. Let's move on to learning about the principles it takes to be all that God wants us to be. First, we need to realize that whatever sport we choose, whether we make it to the pros or not, our playing will ultimately end one day. It's not just about being the best athlete one can become. It's about being the best overall person. That's what an uncommon champion focuses on and realizes. But it doesn't happen by one's self.

REFLECTION QUESTIONS

Questions for athletes:

1. What is your favorite part of competing against others?

2. Have you ever performed poorly and felt like you were unworthy of love due to the performance?

3. If 10 percent of life is what happens to us, what is the other 90 percent?

4. Do you feel you put your identity in what you are as an athlete?

5. Who loves us no matter how we perform?

Questions for parents:

1. Do you have healthy competition with your kids with anything?

2. Do you put your identity in on how great or not so great you may parent?

3. If 90 percent of life is how we respond, how do you respond to your child when they have a bad game?

4. Do you believe that God loves your child even more than you and has a plan for them whether it aligns with your thoughts or not?

CHAPTER 4

Principle One – Finding a Transformational Coach

"Children are apt to live up to what you believe of them."
-CLAUDIA ALTA "LADY BIRD" JOHNSON

C an you think of a time when you were younger and someone looked at you with unconditional and loving eyes? Do you remember ever feeling like you could do no wrong and that no matter what the circumstances, you could run into the arms of a parent, grandparent, or any adult to feel security, love, and acceptance?

Now I want you to imagine the opposite – of feeling like a failure, with no one to turn to. Or feeling abandoned because you didn't perform well enough.

Sports can teach us so much. They can teach us important skills and traits like discipline, commitment, focus, work ethic, teamwork, leadership, respect ... the list can go on and on. On the other side, sports conducted in an unhealthy environment can teach us about the ugliness of manipulation, anger, jealousy, fear, power, judgment, and the shameful feeling of being a failure.

In figure skating, like many sports, young athletes can get lost in the process of going from the adoration of playing a sport to focusing solely on getting approval and acceptance from other human beings. They hear the applause from the audience and feel adored. They work in hopes to win a piece of hardware or a title. This in itself isn't a bad thing. How else would we be able to compete, right? But what we so often mistake is thinking that winning an award must suddenly make one a better person, too. Our culture idolizes "talent;" even if that person's character is still far from ideal.

All too often, coaches, parents, judges, and scouts can use their power to get young athletes to do almost anything they want. But it's not always with the focus to help the athlete. Instead they seem to manipulate upcoming "stars" to get what they want. There's no regard to the development of the athlete. If a child performs well or if a student wins the MVP award at a tournament, then suddenly pride enters these coach's or parent's minds as if they themselves accomplished something.

Development of a whole person unfortunately doesn't seem to be the focus. Instead, continuing to build an athlete to just win and succeed is. Adults can all too often live vicariously through kids as they progress up the ladder of worldly success, regardless how they are developing emotionally or spiritually.

What Transformational Isn't

My parents did an amazing job wanting the best for my sister and myself with our figure skating careers. Whenever our skills or performance would seem to plateau, my parents would seek out the best coaches in the area to keep pushing us to another level. If this meant leaving certain coaches or clubs to begin training at a better facility, we would do so. This allowed my sister and me to train in facilities with some of the best skaters in the world. Through this journey with various training environments and coaches, there was always one thing that seemed to remain the same – transactional coaching. I didn't know it at the time but reflecting on my adolescent and teenage years I can see how the training cultures were strictly transactional. This label of coaching was introduced to me in my adult life through Joe Erhmann in his amazing book, *InsideOut Coaching*. Knowing what I know now, this book should be mandatory for all teachers and coaches to read. Transactional coaching is all about the "X's and O's." It is known to be a style of coaching that focuses solely on one's performance. Some coaches show a student love or praise only when they perform to a certain standard. And, unfortunately, there is little to zero focus on their emotional stability, spiritual wellbeing, or overall character development.

Through the years of my young skating career, this became a staple of how I would feel and adapt to living. If I performed well, then coaches, judges and parents would focus positively on me. If I didn't perform well, then coaches would walk out on my lesson or my parents wouldn't talk to me. Sometimes for days. Or at least it felt like that emotionally. Talk about learning the feeling of shame early on!

As I developed into my teenage years, I entered high school and began to feel the effects of being in my older sister's shadow and having the feeling of not being able to live up to my coach's or parent's expectations. The sport of figure skating already has unbelievable standards, but again, trying to live and perform for love and acceptance of another human being is something that should never be placed on a kid or even an adult. I am curious looking back on my athletic life, now that I know Jesus and God love me no matter what, if my skating career would have been any different. I would like to believe at least my experience through it would have been different!

Colossians 3:23 says, "Whatever you do, work at it with all your heart, as working for the Lord and not for human masters." I wouldn't come to know this verse until years down the road, but I'm certain I would have had it embroidered on my skating bag to remind me who I was working for as I trained and competed. And it wouldn't have been to get love from my coaches or parents anymore. There would have been less tension and worldly pressure to get love, that's for sure!

Unfortunately, I went down other paths to try and find the love that only God can give us. There's a song that says, "Looking for love in all the wrong places." And let me tell you, I did that. Feeling like a failure in a sport and not having much support from adults in my life resulted in me accepting less than ideal relationships and numbing the pain. This is why I believe in Theodore Roosevelt when he said,

"People don't care how much you know until they know how much you care." And if coaches don't show that they care, then they are in the coaching position strictly on the basis to make themselves look and feel better. There needs to be more coaches and teachers that realize the power in their platform and it shouldn't be by using their students to validate themselves as humans.

I now ask myself, "Why didn't my coaches care more about my personal development?" When there was so much focus on the physical training, why wasn't there more integrated training on the emotional, spiritual, and mental areas of a human being? When coaches and teachers have so many hours of opportunity to be with kids on a weekly basis there needs to be more than just "X's and O's" being discussed. These crucial mentors are sometimes spending even more time with kids than their actual parents are through the week. Working toward one's goals has so much more to do than just the physical aspect. Kids need nurturing from those that they are spending time with. Not just beat into them physical demands. Otherwise it is just transactional coaching.

Everyone Needs Mentors

Have you ever heard the quote, "Hurt people hurt people"? A few years into my coaching career, I had another instructor give me unsolicited feedback on how I was coaching. She said, "Stop being a jerk!" Taken back, I went to my car, called a friend, and started bawling. Just like many adverse times in life, I didn't like it in the moment but it ended up being some of the greatest feedback I could have ever received. I'm not condoning the abrupt or slightly aggressive words used to show me my weakness, but it definitely impacted my life. It helped me notice the blind spots that I had in my coaching style.

We don't know what we don't know, right? During my younger years as a coach, especially during individual lessons, I was using the same style of how my parents treated me along with how my figure skating coaches coached me. I was using my authority in all the wrong ways. I was the transactional person that I didn't want to be. I kicked kids off the ice for poor work ethic. Did all I could to make kids vomit, because to the parents of the players that meant I was working them extra hard. I even left kids during lessons, so they could feel the shame that I felt when my coaches or parents left me when I was young. The roles were reversed. And looking back at these situations I just cringe.

I often ask people, "Where did you find your first mentors?" I generally get answers like, "My parents are my mentors," which I quickly respond with, "Sorry, in my mind they can't be." I always encourage people to think outside their network of family members to have more influence for growth. People ask if teachers, pastors, or friends can be mentors. Yes, I believe they can be but it was my first transformational mentor that taught me to look in other possible places. Author and motivational speaker John Maxwell taught me "Successful people find their first mentors in books." Soon after that other coach told me to stop being a jerk, I luckily found a passion for reading books. Thank God!

It was at that point John Maxwell along with Dale Carnegie began to change my life.

With a new sense of awareness of wanting to be a different kind of coach and a more influential leader, I wanted to grow as much as possible. The more I read, unfortunately, the more I began to notice that this kind of drive to learn and grow wasn't very common amongst other coaches. Therefore, this is one of the many reasons I urge parents to know their non-negotiables for someone who will be coaching their kid. Asking coaches simple questions such as "What is the most influential coach you've ever had in your life and why?" Or "What is your favorite book to read to be a better coach?" These can be telltale signs of what kind of influence they will have on their students. If the book is about certain systems or plays, then you will immediately know they are only focused on winning and not developing your child as a better person.

Know Your Non-Negotiables

What are non-negotiables? Think of a time when you were beginning to date or fall in love with someone. What are the values the other person absolutely needed to have for you to continue to date them? Were you looking for a non-smoker and someone of a particular faith? Or maybe you needed them to just be good looking? Are these the same traits that would be acceptable or strong enough values for someone to influence your kid? Maybe the coach does have the kind of faith you want them to have but they may still think it is okay to use swear words as they coach. Or they use shameful, sexist statements in hopes to get a different work ethic. Is that okay? Maybe they don't support the use of drugs but are okay with the statement, "boys will be boys" when it comes to bullying? Knowing your non-negotiables for the coach you choose for your player can be life changing. Whether it is something that will be good or bad is what you need to think about.

In his book, *InsideOut Coaching*, Joe Erhmann talks about two of his role models he uses for his coaching style and urges others to look at their characteristics as well. Being an ex-NFL player, he chooses two people to emulate from some unlikely sources. Erhmann recommends coaches "Seek models outside traditional coaching archetypes and think beyond personal experiences." Who does Erhmann choose to emulate? He describes how he loves Dorothy from the *Wizard of Oz* and Moses from the Bible. How cool is that! He explains how Dorothy is affirming and encouraging rather than demeaning and defaming. Isn't that what you would want for your kid? Combine that with Moses's traits, which as Erhmann says are "based on moral and ethical principles," and we have a transformational coach.

When you learn from Erhmann you go from being a transactional coach, like many of us experienced in our childhood, to following Erhmann's philosophy. Throughout his book, he consistently repeats his creed. Erhmann says, "I am a transformational coach who has a position, power and platform to make a positive difference in the life of my players." He goes on to say, "I coach to help boys become men of empathy and integrity who will lead, be responsible, and change the world for good. I allow for accountability and take responsibility for my actions." This is why I want parents to know their non-negotiables on a deeper level of who they will allow their child to be influenced by. It is so important for coaches to learn from their past, have accountability partners for their actions and to always have mentors to positively influence them.

This is the first principle to what I believe is needed to build uncommon champions. It is common to find coaches and cultures solely focused on winning games. These cultures are everywhere. Coaches and teachers have a greater responsibility and platform than most of them realize. This doesn't mean you shouldn't find coaches who won't help improve your son or daughter's skills. But it shouldn't be the sole focus if you want to create a network for your kid to develop as a whole person. Coaches can still be demanding, yet kind. Critical, yet loving. And there definitely needs to be a focus on accountability for moral behavior but it doesn't need to be shameful. Transformational coaches know that being a coach isn't about them. It's about helping to mold young boys and girls to become better men and women who will be the best brother and sister, best husband and wife and then become even better fathers and mothers that God knows they can be. No one will remember decades later, nor should they care, how many points one got in a championship game compared to what they did to make this world a better place.

Finding a transformational coach will be life changing for your son or daughter. These kinds of coaches will help build better leaders and people by helping their athletes know they are cared for. This will result in greater self-confidence, healthier relationships and knowing they have someone to turn to that cares for their well-being. And I've experienced these kinds of relationships that can go on for decades. Who wouldn't want that for their child?

REFLECTION QUESTIONS

Questions for athletes:

1. Have you ever had a coach that you felt didn't care about you as a person but just someone to perform for them?

2. What characteristic traits define the ultimate coach to you?

3. Do you feel getting an award as an athlete ultimately makes you a better person?

4. Do you ever feel like you perform only to get love and acceptance from others?

5. Who are your mentors to help you become all that you can be?

6. How do you feel you are making the world a better place?

Questions for parents:

1. How are you as a parent preventing your child feeling like they have to perform to get love from you?

2. Have you chosen coaches that care more about developing your child as a person instead of just an athlete?

3. How would you feel as a parent if your child just received an MVP award but found out they were bullying kids on their team or had disrespected the refs in a game?

4. Are you encouraging your kids to find mentors outside the family circle in order to help them grow?

5. What activities are you more focused on with your kids – athletics, academics or helping others?

Chapter 5:

Principle Two through Principle Four

"The only way things are going to
change for you is when you change."
-JIM ROHN, 12 PILLARS

Principle Two - Who Sold You That Philosophy?

I was sixteen years old when I began to really separate myself from my family. I don't remember exactly what I did to get grounded by my parents; it was definitely a moment in my life where I began the "I'll show you" mentality. I believe author and psychologist Angela Duckworth would possibly call this "having grit."

It had just turned spring time in Michigan and I got my car privileges revoked. The problem was that I still had a job that I needed to get to. My parents said they would drive me but only if I paid them.

What?

To me that meant I would have to rely on them which at that time was the last thing I wanted to do. So what would any teenager rebelling against their parents do? I started rollerblading to and from work. Looking back, I don't know how I did what I did. But I believe it was all God. He kept His hand over me during these challenging times. Being a young sixteen-year-old girl, I was rollerblading all alone on busy streets sometimes even leaving work at ten o'clock at night. How I did not trip over the sidewalks was a miracle and crossing the streets without getting hit by a car was clearly a gift from God. And of course, I never wore a helmet. That was the beginning of building grit inside a young woman who would eventually run away from home a few times; grit that ultimately led to my final fate of getting kicked out at age twenty-two. This is when I gained a new mantra that I would repeat to myself daily – failure is not an option.

Why am I telling you this story? Because it is this grit that I learned in my childhood that I want to help instill or expose others to. No, I don't recommend kids getting grounded on purpose or being disrespectful to adults. But I do believe it is our job as coaches, parents, and teachers to not coddle the younger generation. We need to teach them about the importance of adversity. Don't run from struggle but embrace it knowing it will help you grow. In her book, *GRIT: The Power and Passion of Perseverance*, Angela Duckworth says, "Grit is what keeps us focused on our goals. Not for days. Not for weeks. But for months." She goes on to say "To be gritty is to resist complacency."

Grit is what keeps people from giving up or quitting when things get tough. Many people want to believe there is a talent gene when it comes to sports, but it's usually because they want to believe others have more of an edge than they do. I agree with Duckworth when she says genes do play some role in what one will become in life. But it isn't everything. It's pretty tough to be a seven-foot gymnast or four-foot NBA player. But too many people believe successful athletes are just born "naturals."

Duckworth quotes a German philosopher in her book regarding people thinking others are born with more potential than others. Friedrich Nietzsche, says, "Our vanity, our self-love, promotes the cult of genius. For if we think of genius as something magical, we are not obliged to compare ourselves and find ourselves lacking." I would call this denial. Remember, we are all born with great potential, but we must work to bring it out. And it's not just for a few days or a few weeks, but for years.

This is why it's important to have the right philosophy. All too often I work with students who cut corners, don't pay attention to detail, or begin to feel sorry for themselves when things get tough. I turn to them and ask, "Who sold you on that philosophy? Who made you believe you can become all that you can by cheating?" Unfortunately, living in the Western world we are so spoiled. Few kids really understand true struggle. They see the overnight success on social media or the news. Yes, they may hear about how professional basketball players shoot 500 shots a day, or NHL players stick handle for hours, but if they don't see it personally then they don't want to put in the much-needed work themselves. This is why grit plays such a crucial role in reaching goals. It gives athletes that perseverance to keep going especially when the going gets tough, so you can become better than your competitors.

There are many that believe the philosophy of not struggling is what makes one great. They may even see sweat as a sign of weakness. I cringe when I come across these types of attitudes! I usually find it uneasy if I'm not sweating especially if we are training. Author and retired Navy SEAL, Mark Divine, says in his book *The Way of the SEAL: Think Like an Elite Warrior to Lead and Succeed*, "This kind of philosophy of not wanting to struggle is understandable given the level of comfort and wealth we're used to in Western society."

I say we need to run from this kind of thinking! It's about realizing our weaknesses and embracing struggles which is important to get to another level. Divine says, "The keys to satisfaction, excitement, joy and more lie on the other side of a great challenge." It's important to understand that when it comes to training, it's really what our spirits and bodies want to do. Look at little kids. All they want to do is move! You don't see a toddler saying, "Gosh, walking is just too hard. I don't like struggling so I'm just going to stay in the stroller, so mom and dad can push me around for the rest of my life." We need to keep this child-like mindset through our whole lives of wanting to get outside our comfort zone to experience new levels of achievement.

As I tell others, there is no shame in making mistakes. Just be sure to make corrections as you go. It's the only way to learn and grow. And this is where self-confidence is gained, mental toughness is improved, and overall performance goes up by enjoying training and overcoming obstacles. Sounds like buying into the uncommon philosophy of embracing challenges is the way to go wouldn't you say?

Navy SEALS have a saying that I love: "Embrace the suck!" This is an important quote to learn especially when kids or adults don't enjoy training or adversity at first. When kids who have been told how great they are all their lives face struggle for the first time they break down so easily. I remind them, "Embrace the suck!" This can be used during training sessions, losing games, or not making a team. It's really through these moments of "suck" that we are growing and becoming all that God wants us to be. Through consistent training and changing of one's philosophy one begins to enjoy the process needed for true growth because they know the rewards that are coming on the other side. These rewards may not be immediate. Sometimes the rewards may not even be what we initially thought they would be. But the confidence gained through the process and the enjoyment of understanding how to grow is priceless.

So why is it that some stick with their goals and some don't? We've learned about the importance of having transformational coaches in our lives. We see the importance of grit, so we stick with our goals on a daily basis and we don't give up.. But is there more? And how do we become uncommon and not just have what our culture defines as success? Which the majority or common crowd would say is all about one's status and how much money one has. But can't all that be taken away or lost? Therefore, there must be more to one's philosophy than just focusing solely on winning championships, coming in first or beating one's opponent. I would even add these are all achievements which aren't bad in themselves, but being uncommon is more about focusing on fulfillment through one's journey.

Principle Three – Building an Uncommon Culture

Somewhere in the mountains of Vail California, I stood with 26 men. I was the only female who signed up for the 20X Challenge. It was March of 2015; six thirty in the morning; a cold forty-some degrees.

All of a sudden, chaos broke out. We were told to immediately start running to the lake. Following all the other men, I told myself, "It's just like you are with all your hockey boys. You are constantly the only female with players, so there is nothing different about this. You've got this!"

The Navy SEAL coaches were lined up, arms crossed, and some of them even had sunglasses on even though it was barely dawn. Anything to make them appear more intimidating to us, right? It only took less than twenty minutes of us going in and out of the water, doing pushups, and shivering while holding planks. Two men vomited. Coaches were constantly screaming.

I wanted to curl up into a ball and get back to my warm bed.

I generally think of myself as being a mentally tough person, but in this short amount of time I realized what a spoiled human being I am. The luxury of warm water or heat in my house whenever I want it is easily taken for granted. Or to have my fireplace lit while I sit in my nice cozy chair along with being dry instead of soaking wet and shivering really changed my perspective quickly. So here I was, starting a twelve-hour journey that would change my life forever.

SEALFIT's 20X Challenge is a program that was created by retired Navy SEAL Mark Divine. Commander Mark Divine graduated number one in his BUD/S class. He's a pretty remarkable human being. Knowing the dropout rate through Hell Week is extremely high, Divine decided to build a program to help prepare other men to have the emotional resiliency and perseverance to make it through. He then expanded his program to offer training experiences to delusional people like myself who wanted a little taste of what it is like to become a Navy SEAL.

The main reason I was doing the 20X was to learn how to become a better leader. So why not learn from the best of the best? I was told by one of the amazing coaches the 20X Challenge is only 0.01 percent of what they really go through. Yet even with that little percentage the growth in leadership, character, and awareness turned my whole world upside down. They taught me so much more about what it is to be a true teammate, sacrificial leader and be an example of humility, courage and have the traits to building better and stronger relationships.

I sometimes joke with my inner circle that if I was to ever become President of the United States that I would want all parents, teachers, and coaches to go through a 20X challenge like I did. It wasn't until months after completing the 12-

hour challenge that I began to see our culture change by how I led groups in training sessions and what we implemented with teams. It's fascinating how much we really are selfish as human beings and how hard we work to make ourselves appear better to others within our environment. And it's not even being ourselves! How can we build healthy or strong relationships when we have masks on and portraying to others something that we aren't? Can you see why I don't think most commercial gyms and the strength and conditioning industry is doing all they can to help others become all they can be? It's all about being something we aren't and being solely focused on aesthetics. This really needs to change if our next generation is to become all that God knows they can become by growing not just physically but also mentally, emotionally and spiritually through training.

What I learned from the SEALS is a culture of helping one another, not humiliating each other. It's a culture that embraces struggle and has fun with one another while in the midst of adversity. It's a way of life that we should all follow knowing that no one is better than anyone else but instead we all have our own unique gifts to contribute. When we get in touch with our gifts, we perform them better when we stand alongside one another, push one another, and serve one another. This kind of culture allows others to become vulnerable, belong to a community of people who care for one another, and eliminates fear of making a mistake because you know your teammates have your back. What if more families, teams, neighborhoods, schools, and nations followed this? Could you imagine the change in the world?

Let's be uncommon and build this kind of culture which breeds loving relationships, better communication skills and acceptance of everyone's unique gifts.

Learning Life the Navy SEAL Way

Did you know that 55 percent of how we communicate to other human beings is through our body language? One of the first things I learned very quickly from the SEAL coaches was to never put your hands on your hips. Why? Fear is one of the most powerful emotions human beings can feel. Therefore, when we feel fear, most of us will either fold our arms to protect ourselves or put our hands on our hips to make ourselves appear bigger. It's the "I'm bigger and better than you" mentality.

As the SEALS explained to us, it's this kind of mentality that prevents one from learning from others and gets guys killed in the field. EGOs get people killed in their line of work. Maybe something we should all realize! During the 20X, whenever anyone was caught with their hands on their hips everyone was told to drop down and start pushing them out. This meant for us to keep doing pushups until we basically couldn't feel our arms and then the SEALS would bark another order at us.

It's an amazing philosophy. One person doesn't just get punished. Everyone gets punished. Everyone receives the consequences. What's the result? Accountability and morale goes up in the group and there is more teamwork to help those next to you. You begin to stop just thinking about yourself because you don't want any more repercussions due to poor teamwork or egotistical behavior. Don't you think more coaches and teachers should be teaching this? A point I need to make here, though, is that I generally don't like using exercise as a form of punishment. Especially for kids because it causes a negative correlation to something that is actually good for us.

That's why I don't like it when coaches use pushups to punish kids or running them constantly due to a poor performance in a game. What I do like about the SEAL philosophy is it resulted in us having to help one another to correct a poor behavior. We couldn't just focus on ourselves without there being consequences. And *that* is what I loved and believe needs to be taught everywhere to everyone.

Another trait that the SEALS instill is selflessness and humility. No one could leave their assigned swim buddy throughout the whole day. I was once caught being ten feet ahead of my partner and everyone got punished. Another incident was a running exercise. Even if you got done faster than others, we were commanded to go back and run with those finishing. I love this! This philosophy of focusing on others and building a culture of never leaving others is remarkable.

This embodies the philosophy of being created equal and no one is better than anyone else. There was no time to "gloat" about something you just accomplished because others needed help. And isn't that where we find true success and find authentic joy – in helping others? I believe Jesus was kind of smart when he commanded us to "love one another"; which is what the SEAL culture is all about. This is the difference between focusing on just achievement versus fulfillment.

During the 12-hour challenge, the SEALS would say they are more impressed by those that are struggling with something and persevering through it than those who are showing off. If you are a marathon runner then of course you will be great at running. SEALS didn't care about those who were faster or stronger than others but instead enjoyed seeing those who were struggling and kept helping those around them. They knew this took courage and mental fortitude. This is what Commander Mark Divine says is feeding the courage wolf.

What is the courage wolf? Divine teaches that every human being has two wolves in their mind. There is the courage wolf and the fear wolf. Whichever one you feed more will get stronger. If you feed the fear wolf with thoughts of doubt, uncertainty, disbelief then you will become a person who lives in fear and never go outside your comfort zone. If you feed the courage wolf with statements that are strong, loving, and powerful then you will continue to embrace struggles, keep growing as a person and become a better leader and person than you were yesterday.

I often tell others that you can be your best friend or your worst enemy. It's your choice. You can choose your thoughts and what you think about when you are training or when you face adversity. There is a statement I have come across: "Pain is inevitable. Suffering is a choice." One can choose to stay in their comfortable warm bed and never feel pain or they can choose to step out into the real world and learn to feel the pain of being a little colder, the discomfort of training early in the morning and facing the challenges of the day. But you don't have to see it as suffering. When a coach is demanding, or a parent or teacher wants more effort, choose to see it as the pain that is needed for growth. Then you will begin to realize the results that are on the other side of pain are rewards and feelings of getting goals accomplished. Feeding the courage wolf is all about facing uncertainty knowing that one is prepared and ready for anything!

So which wolf are you used to feeding? Are your thoughts getting you closer to your goals or causing unnecessary road blocks? It's important to know that you can control your thoughts but it's equally important to have the right mindset too, which is another key principle into becoming an uncommon champion.

Principle Four – Which Mindset Do You Have?

Psychologist and author Carol Dweck has done amazing research on the two different kinds of mindsets people have. She calls them a fixed mindset and a growth mindset. Which one do you think would correlate to the courage wolf and the fear wolf? In her book *MINDSET: The New Psychology of Success*, Dweck teaches how we can all show a little of each mindset in our lives at different moments. We can show times of being in a fixed mindset which is shown through stubbornness, not listening, or just plain quitting an activity because it's too hard. On the other side of the spectrum, we can show perseverance and mental toughness with a growth mindset by welcoming challenges, listening to feedback from others, and having a willingness to keep working on problems. It's important to have as much of a growth mindset as possible to reach our potential.

So, what are some other examples of having a fixed or growth mindset? When I work with younger kids around the age of six to eight years old I'll tell them I have a certain drill for them but then joke that it may be too hard for them or that they may not be able to handle it.

"Oh, I don't know if you can do this, Johnny. It may just be too hard for you to jump over those cones," I'll tease.

"I can do it! Let me know show you!" Johnny will say as he eagerly skates towards the cones.

One of the characteristics of having a growth mindset is knowing that skills and intelligence can grow through work. Growth mindset kids believe there are no fixed traits or fixed IQ's. We can all keep growing! Therefore, when there are setbacks or mistakes made, which is inevitable, growth mindsets just get up and keep going. Usually with a smile on their face too! They know they are a work in progress and it is all part of their journey.

When it comes to fixed mindsets, I often see these behaviors in the teenage years of athletes and especially with the "prima donnas" I've been exposed too. You know the ones who just think they are greater than God himself? When players think they are the best player in the world just because they are the best player on a low-level team it only sets them up for disaster. It's the "big fish in a small pond" syndrome.

As a figure skater, I never had to worry about this problem. We are always watching the best in the world compete on television or we know what maneuvers we need to perform to get to another level. There isn't much room in figure skating for a big EGO; you are falling every day and struggling to get that "perfect" score. Hockey, on the other hand, is a breeding ground for EGOs, delusion, and fixed mindsets.

I remember a time when I was working with a handful of NHL players. They called me to work on their skating. When they began to struggle, one threw a stick across the ice and another stepped in front of me to coach another player as if he knew more than me and I had to constantly remind them struggling didn't mean they were failing. "Falling isn't failing" is a quote I constantly have to remind the fixed mindsets about. With higher level players, I just can't believe the lack of maturity or little desire to want to improve when I expose them to their weaknesses. Instead, what do most fixed mindsets do? They quit lessons and the training. One NHL player even told me he was mad he couldn't do the drills. And he *still* quit! These are examples of how having a fixed mindset can cause even those at the highest levels to not improve even more because they instead just want to be praised for how good they already are.

Growth mindsets are inspired by the greatness in others. Fixed mindsets only want to validate their talent. This means acting like a superstar. I was so confused when athletes called me to work on their skating, but they didn't want to struggle. So many kids and athletes want to be around those who will just validate who they are. But this is the worst thing for them. Dweck has learned that even though kids want to be praised it hinders their growth. It harms their motivation and it harms their performance. Why?

I love it when I get to explain this research to kids, especially to those who think I'm a jerk for giving them constructive feedback. All I'm trying to do is help them! Dweck has learned from her extensive research that even though praise may boost one's self-esteem, it only lasts for a moment. If one is constantly praised from coaches and parents, the second they hit a difficult math problem in school, or a drill in hockey or struggle with doing a pull-up, their confidence drops and their motivation is lost. All of a sudden, they wrap their identity into that struggle and begin to believe they are a failure.

Dweck believes we need to praise work ethic, not one's skills or intelligence. She warns us to stay away from telling a child how smart they are or how talented they are because, again, this risks them quitting when they face adversity. Remember, there is no finish line to success or one's growth. Just like the Navy SEALS believe we can always do more, strive for more and keep pushing our limits. We need to have growth mindsets to believe in the journey of always wanting to be better than we were yesterday.

Therefore, in becoming an uncommon champion we have now learned from the Navy SEALS that we need to believe in the right philosophy of not cutting corners but instead run wholeheartedly toward struggles and weaknesses. We need to be part of a culture that embraces the suck, shows humility, and helps hold others accountable. It's great to accomplish certain goals, but we must remember to encourage those around us to become their best as well. Remember, it's common for others to cut corners. It's common for most people to want to be praised for what they accomplish. It's even common to bully, shame others and even use less than ideal language. If being uncommon was easy, then everyone would do it.

Carol Dweck taught us that it's having a growth mindset that helps us embrace the changes needed to get to another level and to have the mental toughness to get critical feedback from other. This is also part of what Commander Mark Divine reminds us to do which is feed the courage wolf. There may be people one day who may tell you that you aren't capable of something or that your goals are too high. It's your choice if you are going to believe them or not. Be your best friend, not your worst enemy. Become that champion you were meant to be.

Remember, we can always get better every day and it is through these daily challenges that true confidence will emerge. It is not through titles or a certain status or how many goals one scores; it's knowing at the end of the day you gave your best to become all that God wants you to become. There is a saying that tells us "Watch your thoughts, they become words; watch your words, they become actions; watch your actions they become habits; watch your habits, they become character; watch your character, for it becomes your destiny." Character in my mind is everything, and if we're not careful other people will shape it for us.

So, let's move on to see what uncommon character really looks like.

REFLECTION QUESTIONS

Questions for athletes:

1. What experiences have helped you gain GRIT?

2. Do you feel you have GRIT that will help you day in and day out for years to come to reach your goals?

3. How do you feel about challenges? Do you focus on the pain or the rewards you will gain after?

4. Fifty-five percent of how we communicate to others is through what?

5. What kind of body language do Navy SEALS dislike because it comes off as if you think you are better than everyone else?

6. What are the two different kinds of mindsets according to Carol Dweck?

7. What does Carol Dweck suggest we praise instead of skills or IQ?

Questions for parents:

1. How do you show that you have grit to your kids?

2. What physical and mental challenges do you embrace with your kids in order to grow together?

3. How do you feel about having better body language like the SEALs follow?

4. Where do you show the most growth mindset in your life to be an example to your kids?

5. Do you praise your kid's success, talents, smarts or their effort?

CHAPTER 6:

Principle Five – Character

"While we teach, we learn."
-SENECA

I stood before a boys' high school hockey team and cited one of the most powerful verses in scripture. Luke 16:10 says, "Whoever can be trusted with very little can also be trusted with much, and whoever is dishonest with very little will also be dishonest with much."

Their team had won a State Championship the year before. They were hoping to make another run for the trophy, but had just embarrassed the coaches, their families, and myself due to some poor choices over the weekend.

This team was familiar with hearing how important the little things are in life. It's the little things that add up to the big things. The previous Saturday the team was playing in a special game outside in downtown Detroit. The head coach was super excited about the day. The sun was shining.

Friends and family were all gathered around the outdoor arena to watch two teams face off in what is a rare occasion in hockey. The feeling of joy didn't last for very long though.

The head referee of the game had just told our team's coach that if any of his players didn't have their mouth guards they would be ejected from the game. Some of the best players on the team including the captain got caught not having this pivotal piece of equipment. So, what did they choose to do? They went into the locker room and put hockey tape on their teeth and cut mouth guards in half to share with one another. They were lying and trying to get away with something because they weren't properly prepared.

They overlooked the little things. They may have tricked the referee but luckily the head coach – being a transformational coach – saw a teaching moment and sat them for the rest of the game. He didn't care about winning or losing. Instead he knew these boys needed to understand consequences, regardless of whether their friends and family were in the stands.

I asked the teammates why no one said anything. "Where was the accountability?" I asked. The Navy SEALS would have had a field day with them because it's not only the person who failed to prepare properly who's at fault but the ones next to them who allowed this to happen. If you love one another then hold each other accountable. Speak the uncomfortable truth to each other in love. Not only does this build leadership and confidence, it's also showing selflessness by looking out for one another. Accountability is too often seen as ratting someone out or tattle tailing in our society.

The outlook on this needs to change. When we learn to embrace accountability I believe more trusting relationships will be built and less bullying will happen as well.

We were six weeks from the State finals and I told them they didn't have the character or discipline to win another championship. Again, "If you can't be trusted with a little then you can't be trusted with much." After pointing out their lack of character and accountability, I told them to prove me wrong. I love to be proven wrong, especially when it works in the other person's favor for growth. Six weeks later the boys were holding the championship trophy over their heads again just like the previous year. When they got into the locker after the game one of the players remembered my challenge and asked, "Who's going to call Jennifer and tell her we just proved her wrong?"

So how did this team do it again? How do teams not just win championships but become uncommon? It's all about character. In his book *Letters from Leaders: Personal Advice for Tomorrow's Leaders from the World's Most Influential People*, Henry O. Dormann compiled letters written by many different leaders from around the world offering wisdom to the next generation. One of his letters is by the chairman at the time of Viacom, Sumner Redstone. I love Redstone's advice. He says, "Opportunity does not knock, but with his 'Three C's,' you can go out and grab it." What are his "Three C's?" Redstone says in regard to opportunity, "It's a matter of competence, commitment, and character. But without character, I'm not interested in competence and commitment." Therefore, it is vital to keep building one's character as we continue our journey.

Author and speaker Jim Rohn says we are the average of the five people we hang around with most. I often ask my students, "On a scale of 1 to 10, Hitler being a 1 and Jesus Christ being a 10, which one do you want to be?" They all want to be a 10. But how do we get there? It is so important to know that who we choose to hang around with will be our circle of influence. But it's not just who we hang out with. It's also what music we are listening to, what books we are reading, television shows we watch and movies we are okay with going to see. All these leave imprints on our subconscious mind and begin to mold our character. Don't think this is true? Then the advertising business wouldn't be a billion-dollar business due to how much influence it has on the choices we make!

Dr. Tim Elmore talks about this in his leadership teachings. Elmore has created an amazing line of work through his books titled *Habitudes: Images that Form Leadership Habits and Attitudes*. In his teachings, Elmore explains the GIGO principle: "Leaders don't feed on garbage, because they know the GIGO principle: garbage in, garbage out." He goes on to say, "Leaders work hard at investing the right material inside themselves and avoid the wrong material, so that what comes out is right!"

It's important to understand our brains are like laptops. What kind of language we are around, what images we see are stored into our brain like a hard drive on a computer. It's not easy to build strong character and sometimes we must even change the group of friends we hang out with which takes courage. We need to be aware of what type of person we want to become and then choose our friends wisely. Usually the choices we need to make to become our best selves are usually the unpopular choices to make. But that's because most people want to choose the easy route in life. But remember being uncommon isn't so common.

We discussed earlier the importance of finding a transformational coach. These coaches should be helping students learn the principles just discussed along with teaching how important it is for teammates and friends to be holding each other accountable. I learned from Jim Rohn that there are no successful hermits. We all need accountability partners. If the road to becoming uncommon was easy, then everyone would be more successful. It takes having a growth mindset, mental toughness and the humility to not just hold others accountable but to receive that accountability as well. It's a remarkable sight when I get to see a team working together to build one another up and to help one another. The listening skills go up, the moral goes up, integrity goes up and the result is so much more joy and confidence. But there is still more.

Building Trust

As I mentioned, there are no successful hermits. We all need others to help us grow. What's amazing about this concept is God created humans to be in community with each other. Scripture says, "It's not good for man to be alone" (Genesis 2:18). Trust is an important factor in relationships. Not just between two people, but within teams, organizations, tribes, nations, etc. But how is trust built? You can't just command someone to trust you, right? There needs to be certain actions that happen and some lead to building trust faster between people than others.

You may have heard about companies who do team building exercises such as trust falls. Yet, when I was learning from the Navy SEALS they didn't talk about doing any of those things. I haven't heard of much success with these kinds of team building exercises either. On the other hand, though, what I have learned about is the importance of touching one another. You may be wondering "how does touching my teammate or coworker build trust? And isn't that kind of weird or invading their space?"

Author and motivational speaker Michael Massucci explains one of the reasons why basketball player Steve Nash is so successful. Massucci, the author of *An Elite Journey: A Young Man's Leadership Story*, teaches teams about how Steve Nash, on average, gives 239 high-fives per games. Don't think that is a lot? Try giving a 100 high-fives in one day let alone 239 in 2 hours! Why is something like a high-five so helpful? One could say it's about encouragement or acknowledging another person, but it's much more than that.

Research says that when we touch each other it releases the happy-feeling hormones known as oxytocin and serotonin. These hormones are increased when mothers give birth. They are also released when we hug one another because of the human connection. And it's through this human connection of touch we build something as powerful as trust with one another.

We have seen teams who train with us not only begin to love one another more because of the high-five culture, but they become over-all more joyful as they train and practice with one another. All through a few high-fives! Other results are healthy competition between teammates, enjoyment of another person's success and holding each other accountable out of love. High-fives build better cultures and they also help win games. I challenge teams I work with that the team that gives more high-fives to each other will most likely be the one that comes out on the winning side.

And we have seen this happen repeatedly. This doesn't mean that simple high-fives will just automatically result in a Stanley cup championship, but the least they will do is build trust and love among teammates and more enjoyment in playing a game they love. Could you imagine if schools and teachers started implementing this with their students? Maybe more kids would become friends, there would be less kids sitting alone in the lunchrooms and my ultimate dream would be no more bullying because we would all begin to see we are all created equal out of love. Are you with me to start this movement?

What Does God Hate the Most?

So why don't we see more high-five cultures out in the world? Why do I have such a hard time implementing this principle and seem to get pushback even after such proven results? I often ask people what God hates the most. I'll get answers like sin, lying, murder. Which, yes, the Bible says are all bad. But there's one thing in particular that comes up over and over again that God detests. Proverbs 16:5 states, "The Lord detests all the proud of heart."

Maybe you've heard of a more common statement which is pride comes before the fall. This is when one thinks that they are better than everyone else and they don't follow any moral codes, which leads them to soon fall from their status and success. We have plenty of examples in sports, business and politics which have proven this time and time again.

Scripture warns us against pride and about being boastful. Years ago, I came across an acronym regarding the word EGO. It said, "EGO means one is Edging. God. Out." Being in a male dominated sport with a focus on how fast and powerful one can be, I come face to face all too often with those that think they are better than everyone else. I've even had people tell me they think they even need an EGO to be successful. It's funny how this is the total opposite of what the Navy SEAL philosophy is or what having strong character looks like. And one summer after years of coaching in an industry and culture that seems to reward egotistical behavior I had finally had enough.

I had just gone through nine weeks of intensive training with students. It was one of my greatest summers with coaching, but it was about to turn into one of the hardest moments of my life. I was sending students that I love off to their next academic year and hockey season. I handed out books to those going into college and gave out heartfelt cards to the seniors of the program. This was an action that I loved to do to give words of encouragement and also show students how much they meant to me. What I didn't realize was I was about to feel humiliation from those I thought were my leaders as well as some of the strong character students in the program.

What was supposed to be a moment of love, trust, and support turned into a handful of athletes showing what author Ryan Holiday would say is, "The disease of me." Up until this moment, I didn't realize some of the athletes were speaking poorly about the program and about the coaching. It's as if they thought they were better than everyone else, including me who helped them get stronger, faster and scholarships to schools. Martin Luther King Jr. once said, "The ultimate measure of a man is not where he stands in moments of comfort and convenience but where he stands at times of challenge and controversy."

This is what I love about training and challenges. It shows a person's true colors, especially the more challenging the training is. Knowing the importance of character and wanting the best program around I knew I couldn't keep certain athletes who were not supportive, couldn't handle the demands of the program or lacked the values to want to be a better person. Nothing taught me more in that moment, though difficult at the time, how important it is to focus primarily on building strong character athletes and people.

When we allow students to have poor values, EGOs or if they think they have already made it, we aren't doing our part to help them become the best they can be. And sometimes it takes tough love to stand for what you believe in regardless of what our society says. Remember, being a transformational coach isn't about status or whom one is working with, but instead, about caring for the overall development of the person. Most transactional coaches don't reprimand their athletes, especially their "best" athletes because they are too worried about wins and losses and making themselves look better. Finding a transformational coach is per se "transformational" on your kid's journey toward success because they will make sure to keep their students humble knowing it's about what kind of person one is becoming, not just what kind of athlete they are becoming.

Pride is one of the most frustrating traits I have had to put up with being in this industry. I've seen it keep kids from growing, causing them to treat others poorly and to never reach their goals. No wonder God hates it so much! Luckily, it was learning from Navy SEALs of the importance of remaining humble, helping others and what true leadership looks like that has given me so many tools to build a culture to transform others and help them reach their goals. What's amazing about the SEALs' focus on selflessness is it's what our true self wants to do.

It makes me wonder, at what point in our lives do we lose this capacity to want to help others that are around us? Why do I see all too often people who are brought up thinking the world revolves around them? Fortunately, I have found a formula which when implemented brings us back to our genuine selves of being created for a purpose of being here to help and serve others.

Who are you helping?

When we are done with certain drills or in the middle of a training session, I always ask, "Who is still working?" When part of our team may not yet be finished with a skill then all of us should still be working or encouraging and helping others to finish well. A common acronym for TEAM is, "Together. Everyone. Accomplishes. More." And guess what, life is a team sport! This shouldn't just happen at a hockey rink or on a soccer field, but what about in the classroom, board room and high school lunchrooms? We seriously need to get rid of people's EGOs. We need to help others take off their masks, to love on one another and work more as a team. No matter where we are. Why can't we teach kids more to help each other everywhere?

Our EGO is the false part of ourselves that causes us to be delusional and will keep us from becoming all that we can be. It is the part of ourselves that causes us to think everyone else is here to serve me. EGOs make us think we don't need to keep improving, or we shouldn't show others that we struggle. Yet, how can that kind of thinking help us grow when it is through struggling that we improve? When we are humble and realize we are not God and that there will always be things we can learn, then we will progress faster in our sport and in life. Author Brené Brown talks about how this is what true courage looks like by embracing weakness. It's through vulnerability and letting others see our struggles that is the ultimate measure of courage. And it's in these moments we are serving others by letting ourselves be seen because then they can help us in the process. It's doing life together rather than all alone. When we train with one another, there should be no technology allowed. No phones, no televisions, and no music. Being distracted is, to me, why so many feel alone and isolated. It's the opposite of helping one another.

This concept of getting rid of the EGO correlates with having the growth mindset as well. Carol Dweck interviewed many different athletes and discussed their traits in her book *Mindset*. One athlete is Mia Hamm. She points out that when interviewing this world-class soccer player, she learned that Hamm never thought of herself as the greatest player in the world. Hamm told her, "And because of that, [Not thinking I was the best] then someday I might be." That is strong character. That is humility. That's staying EGO-less.

Marcus Aurelius said once, "It can only ruin your life if it ruins your character." When we begin to experience some small success, it will be easy for our EGO to want to take over and tell us how great we are. Our friends may want to praise our skills and parents will smother us in love and affection. It's important to seek out those who will continue to point out where else we can keep growing, keep us humble and keep building our character. I understand that it's great to win awards and score a lot of goals. And guess what? I've seen a lot of jerks do this. I've seen greedy and selfish people get called up to higher levels, to get nominated as captains on their team and find a lot of worldly success. It's common to see this. But I am here to ask you what kind of person do you want to be? What are you doing to make the world a better place? Do you want your tombstone to say, "Scored the game winning goal," or do you want it to say, "World's kindest, most generous person known to the world?" Which will you choose?

In his book *Ego is the Enemy*, Ryan Holiday says, "Reflecting on what went well or how amazing we are doesn't get us anywhere." He goes on to say, "We must subsume our EGO and smash it with continually higher standards." There is no finish line. Our EGO will want to tell us that we have already "arrived." But it's that kind of mentality which keeps people from wanting to keep working or keep improving. This is what keeps people from getting to the highest level possible. Trust me. I've seen this problem a thousand times. One could say this is what common looks like.

Therefore, be the one who embraces the Navy SEAL philosophy of building a culture of humility. Have strong character traits such as selflessness, courage, respect for others, accountability and building trust through high-fives and love. Be the uncommon. It really is what God created us to be and what our bodies and spirits want. Don't be selfish. Don't be prideful. It may feel good in the moment but it's those types of character traits that God hates the most. Scripture says, "Do not be conformed to this world." This will lead to living a more authentic life resulting in building a culture of trust between others, building deeper relationships, and having stronger values. Character determines one's destiny and it's through character we base our life decisions. Strong character people aren't easily pressured into poor choices. They choose the hard right versus the easy wrong which will lead to better outcomes in their life. Whether it's academically, athletically, relationally, and spiritually. Therefore, leave common for someone else, and be the uncommon champion God knows you can be.

REFLECTION QUESTIONS

Questions for athletes:

1. From the book, *Letters from Leaders*, we learned about the importance of three C's. Which one is the most important?

2. What are we the average of?

3. What behavior does Steve Nash do to increase his team morale and build trust?

4. What does God hate the most?

5. Do you think we need an EGO to be successful?

6. What does an EGO cause us to do regarding how we think about ourselves?

7. What does the acronym T.E.A.M. stand for?

8. Do you help others when you finish your classwork, yardwork, drills, etc.?

Questions for parents:

1. Who or what do you feel is shaping your kid's character the most in their life?

2. Are you willing to implement more high-fives and hugs with one another to deepen your relationship with your kids?

3. Did you hug and high-five your parents, teachers or coaches growing up?

4. Where has pride caused you to fall in your life or prevented you from becoming all that God knows you can become?

5. How do you help your child see how pride can prevent us from growing?

6. How do you help your child create better habits in helping others rather than it just being "chores"?

CHAPTER 7:

Principle Six – Breathing

"Every breath is a prayer.
Every breath is a blessing."
-DAN BRULÉ, JUST BREATHE

There we were lined up on the sandy beaches of Encinitas, California. We were told to lock arms with the people next to us. After what seemed liked doing a hundred pushups in the sand the SEALs yelled for us to walk into the ocean side by side with each other. We were knee deep into the ocean when they yelled, "Stop! Now turn around lay down on your backs and stay there!"

Now you would think it would be warm and relaxing to lay down and catch some rays from the sun. Nothing could be further from the truth. It only took one wave coming over the top of my head for the panic to set in. I was locked arms with those next to me which only made me feel more pulled down under the waves. I was forced to stay there. If you've never laid down with waves constantly coming over your head trying to keep your head above water, then I suggest you do this exercise. I was struggling to stay calm. I kept trying to turn my head to prepare for the next wave, but it never seemed to be long enough for me to catch my breath. I seriously thought I was going to drown.

Flailing around seeing the panic in my eyes there was a SEAL who kept looking at me and telling me to breathe. Over and over again, he would look at me with calm in his eyes and just say, "Breathe." Then, to keep our minds off the cold someone down the line started to get the group to sing. I'm not kidding you. And I couldn't believe it myself. I thought, "What? You want me to sing? Seriously, what in the world are we doing? Who in their right minds lies down in the freezing cold water, locked arms with others and then begins to sing the tune row, row, row your boat?"

I suppose it was to help us to breathe, make it more fun or get our minds off the negative. But it was right then when I couldn't take it anymore. All of a sudden, the ocean's waves somehow began to pull a group of about fifty of us out to sea! This would be a moment I'll never forget which showed how selfish I was as a human. I unlocked my arms of my swim buddies next to me, stood up and ran back to the dry land. Just as I got to the beach a coach got in my face, pointed to the ocean, and yelled, "Get back with your crew, Matras!" It's crazy regardless of how nervous or scared I was of drowning, when there's a 200-pound SEAL yelling at you like that you will do what you are told!

I shamefully got back next to my partners, lied down and locked arms with them again. We were then immediately told to get up and run to the next point of our challenge which was about a half mile down the beach. We gathered together as a group. The coaches kept telling us to get closer and closer. My body was uncontrollably shivering from the cold. The coaches were getting us closer to use our bodies as heat and then telling us to focus on our breath. This was the beginning of the journey which would teach me about the number one tool God has given us in our toolbox that if we work on improving the efficiency of it we can improve our chances of reaching our potential. What is the tool? Breathing.

What We Have All Wrong

I remember when I was younger there would be moments before getting on the ice to compete and I would constantly yawn. I would be worried if I was tired. So many people say, "Wake up!" They think yawning is a sign of being fatigued. Or what's another statement associated with yawning? "Am I boring you?" When we are brought up with these beliefs about yawning, we then begin to suppress them or hide the very thing our bodies want to do. Why are we not giving ourselves permission to be fully human? No wonder we're so unhealthy and limiting what we can do!

It was at the Unbeatable Mind Retreat in San Diego where I first met the world-renowned expert in breathing, Dan Brulé. It was amazing to hear him speak and destroy all the myths about asthma, yawning and explain the importance of conscious breathing. During his talk, I believe I yawned more in that hour than I did the last decade of my life. I am curious, if we are told there's something so wrong about yawning then what else are we getting incorrect that's keeping us from all that we can become in life?

In his book *Just Breathe: Mastering Breathwork for Success in Life, Love, Business, and Beyond*, Dan Brulé says, "Science is finally taking a more serious look at the phenomenon of yawning and why it's contagious." He goes on to say, "The yawning reflex lights up the same part of our brain that is associated with empathy, bonding, play and creativity."

Instead of fighting what our bodies want to do we need to embrace it. And not just half yawns but full body yawns which make our mouths open wide and eyes water. Brulé explains that this helps improve one's health through massaging of the lymphatic system and it is a powerful neural-enhancing tool. This is a simple way to begin improving one's breathing and overall performance. So next time anyone comments about you yawning and that you're being impolite you can tell them you are doing what your body wants to do. Also, note that neuroscientists can't find any other single activity that has so many benefits for our health and well-being. Isn't that amazing?

Dan Brulé works with Navy SEALs, hostage extraction teams, Olympians, blade fighters and many others on conscious breathing. Breathing is the number one way to improve health, focus, creativity, and one's ability to stay calm. Warriors are taught these amazing techniques with breathing because they deal with life and death situations.

Commander Mark Divine and Dan Brulé are doing their best to teach these simple techniques to the rest of the world so we can improve our overall health, awareness, and performance. This is why I teach it to as many athletes and teams because of the results it can produce. Therefore, I am on a mission to get more teachers and coaches to understand this phenomenon and encourage kids to do full body yawns whenever their bodies are calling for it.

How about you? Do you want to learn how to manage your emotions and mental state to become all that you can be? An easy way to learn how to improve your breathing is through what Mark Divine calls box breathing. It's what he uses to stay calm and practices before firefights, engagement with enemies, and also after missions. This is what he walked us through while at the Unbeatable Mind retreat in California and what I practiced for months before going through my 20X Challenge. Box breathing is making a box with one's breathing pattern. Divine taught us with a four count but there are many other advanced techniques one can learn as well. Pause for a moment and do this exercise with me.

Sitting as tall as you can in a chair or standing upright with your shoulders back and down bring your focus and attention to your breathing. Expel all the air out of your lungs. Now inhale slowly while counting to four. Pause for the count of four, staying in a relaxed state. Then exhale for the count of four. And again, pause for the count of four. Inhale slowly to the count of four. Pause and relax at the top of the inhale for the count of four. Then exhale slowly for four counts as if gradually letting air out of a balloon. Then hold the breath again at the bottom of the exhale for four counts. You are making a box or square with an even four-count.

To find more information on box breathing, go to www. unbeatablemind.com.

When I first began to practice box breathing, I had a hard time holding at the bottom, which Divine says is normal. That is our body's way of telling us we don't know how to breathe deeply. The more I practiced the more I improved. But let me tell you it wasn't easy; you must be disciplined with practicing it consistently throughout the day. Just like anything else in life, right? You won't get better unless you make up your mind to do the work. And to think, this is a free way of automatically taking one's game and life to a whole other level. Forget all the marketing toward supplements or sport enhancing drinks. God already gave us the best performance enhancing drug there is – oxygen! You just need to learn how to use it through keeping an open mind and working at conscious breathing during your daily activities.

All too often when we tell people in America the benefits of meditation they say they don't have the time to practice something like that. Or it's something that only yogis or guru's do. Dan Brulé says you can practice breathing anywhere and at any time. And guess what? It is a form of meditation. I now find my body automatically working on deeper breathing when in the car, on the phone, in training sessions and even when I wake up in the middle of the night.

Going through one or two rounds of box breathing before even getting out of bed, is a great way to start the day.

Connect that breathing with a strong statement, a heartfelt prayer, or a strong word for the day, and you are more likely to have a great day! We teach this practice to kids and so many of them say they use it before taking tests, between shifts in a hockey game and when stressed out. I go through at least one round of box breathing before I get out of the morning and connect it to my mantra which is, "Let's do this, God!" What will you choose for your statement?

Have you ever heard of the statement, "Families that pray together stay together"? I believe that families or teams that breathe together stay together and perform better together. Have you ever just rested next to someone and breathed with them, synchronizing your breathing pattern with each other? I challenge you to do it. Get vulnerable and breathe with someone. It really is transformational. Breathing together as a group creates a deeper bond and connection. It's cool to have kids eagerly ask us if we will be doing box breathing at the end of training sessions. Our bodies want to breathe deeper and as Brulé says our breathing affects everything else in our lives. He says, "If you need to control yourself – your mind, body, emotions, posture, or behavior – then start by getting control of your breathing." I love that!

We need to teach our bodies to lead with the breath and if we ever feel like we are hitting a limit, physically, mentally or emotionally, then we need to bring ourselves back to the breath. Too many kids tell me how their parents have road rage. I tell them to teach their parents box breathing. What else is there better to do when you are stuck in traffic or on a long drive? Practice breathing, yawning, and learning how to be grateful is a great way to pass the time instead of having unnecessary rage at another human driving. Don't you agree?

Focusing on our breathing helps us to stay calm during many moments in life especially when we think we may be dying during a hard training session. When we are pushed outside our comfort zone and feel like we can't catch our breath we just need to consciously breathe! Our brains are meant to protect us and when we feel pain, struggle, or fear then we tend to hold our breath. We need to retrain our bodies by practicing box breathing to take our work capacity, strength, and power to another level. Our thoughts may go toward the negative with pain which causes us to do short, rapid breaths. When we think something sucks or if we are afraid all we need to do is breathe to get us through it. With more conscious breath training we can keep pushing our limits resulting in greater outcomes. Not just in sports, but in school and in life. This will result in greater awareness of ourselves, deeper connection with our own bodies and allow us to control our thoughts during adverse moments. Maybe there would be less fighting between others, improved emotional resiliency and greater opportunities to grow just by connecting ourselves with our breath more. Doesn't that sound amazing?

In *Just Breathe*, Brulé interviews a gentleman by the name of Mikhail Ryabko. He is a world-renown martial arts master. Ryabko encourages others to do breath-hold training to become more comfortable with being uncomfortable.

He says, "Learn to relax and tolerate air hunger." These are great practices and words of wisdom, especially when one is being double shifted, pushing one's limits in training or doing something that might be fearful. Get comfortable with discomfort by controlling your breath. Brulé suggests if you want to get better at being comfortable when you are feeling discomfort from struggling to catch your breath, work on box breathing with making the hold at the bottom longer by one second each day.

Don't just inhale right away, but instead work on not giving in to the "urgency" to want to inhale but hold it longer. It's important to stay relaxed though and give yourself grace if it doesn't come easily to you. I'm still working to improve this. It will be a life-long journey, but I believe the younger we can get kids to learn this, the faster we can create a culture of positivity and a world full of more peace.

One last thing I want to mention regarding breathing is regarding the Navy SEALs. Did you know Navy SEALs on average can hold their breath underwater for 4 minutes? The world record for holding one's breath is over 22 minutes. When I tell my students this I find it funny when we are 20 minutes into a training session and I look at the clock and see they are struggling to breathe, I mention how the world record holder would still be holding his breath! It really is about what one is focusing on! Instead of letting thoughts wonder and thinking something is too hard or allowing fear or doubt to enter one's mind, all we have to do is bring our focus and awareness back to our breath. Simple concept but it will go nowhere without you putting in the work!

Remember, we all have certain self-imposed limits that we need to remove to become our best selves. If they are self-imposed then that means we can self-remove them! And the best way to get started is through breath work. Box breathing, which is the practice of breath control, is necessary for anyone who wants to become uncommon. Practice conscious breathing before getting out of bed, before training, before taking a test and teach it to everyone you know. You will see your focus improve, ability to stay calm will be easier, performance will progress faster and the ability to face challenges in all areas of your life will come more naturally knowing that the connection to your Creator is only one breath away.

REFLECTION QUESTIONS

Questions for athletes:

1. What is the number one tool that God has given us in our toolbox that if we don't practice it we will never reach our potential?

2. What have neuroscientists found as the most beneficial single activity for our bodies?

3. What does Commander Mark Divine do before and after missions which he encourages us to work on daily to improve our focus, creativity and overall performance?

4. What is the world record for someone holding their breath under water?

Questions for parents:

1. Do you think working on one's breathing is a waste of time or do you believe it can truly enhance one's health, performance, focus, and emotional control?

2. Have you ever been told that yawning is rude and instead suppressed it?

3. How will you begin to implement box breathing or yawning more as a family?

4. How will you hold each other accountable to begin and end each day with conscious breathing and connecting that to a mantra or an intention for the day?

5. Have you ever just held your child or a loved one and breathed with them?

6. Do you believe how you breathe affects those around you?

CHAPTER 8:

Principle Seven – Be Deliberate!

"Today I will do what others won't so tomorrow I can do what others can't."

-JERRY RICE

During my earlier years of figure skating, I was with a coach who was a little more on the fun side. It was like she was more focused on being my friend than getting me to another level. At the time, we didn't understand why I wasn't winning many competitions, even if I was still doing challenging jumps for my level. My sister was with a different coach than me and was excelling well – so well that the coach finally told my parents that maybe it was time for her to move on to a different club to help push her even more.

As we moved to another rink with more advanced coaching and higher-level athletes, I chose a male coach who was pivotal for my career. There's a quote that states, "If you do not consciously create good habits then you unconsciously create bad ones." What this new coach was about to teach me was my jumping technique was all wrong. I had created bad habits with poor coaching and now had to relearn how to jump correctly. With a new coach, new habits, and better performances I was on track to winning competitions and even going on to win championships and compete nationally. What was the difference? The kind of practice which in research has shown to be critical to becoming the best we can be.

When I retired from my figure skating career and got into coaching hockey players, I couldn't believe all the deficiencies in their skating. Well, no wonder they had so many bad habits! All the hockey coaches I came across just skated players as fast as they could around in circles and up and down the ice. This kind of practice wasn't helping them regardless of how hard they felt they were working. To paraphrase Geoff Colvin: there was no deliberate practice. When I began to work with hockey players I wanted the players to go slower, focus on their strides, get proper leg extension, enhance their edges, and increase their body awareness. The majority of them absolutely hated this. Many athletes still hate this kind of practice. Why is this? First, let's explain what deliberate practice isn't.

When you go to the driving range for hours and practice only hitting your driver as far as possible, this isn't deliberate practice. When you and your friends go to open skate or sticks and pucks for hours, this isn't deliberate practice. Doing bench pressing, bicep curling, or anything that isn't taxing on the mind would not be considered deliberate practice. In his book, *Talent Is Overrated*, Geoff Colvin explains what the experts and professionals do in order to reach that kind of world-class status. He explains beautifully what deliberate practice is. He says, "It can actually be described as a recipe for not having fun."

Not having fun? Huh, oh! Most kids just want to have fun, right? Colvin says, "Deliberate practice is insistently seeking out what we're not good at. Then identify the painful, difficult activities that will make us better and do those things over and over until we're mentally exhausted." Sounds like we are going to have to have a lot of grit and a growth mindset to accomplish this!

I don't know about you, but I am never mentally exhausted after screwing around at the driving range or sticks and pucks or anything that isn't difficult. It's also vital that in order to grow we get feedback from others during our deliberate practice. This is why it's so important to have a growth mindset. If one has a fixed mindset, they will only see feedback as criticism or an attack on them personally. No wonder I get so many kids who never come back to me and just decide to seek out things that are easier. Did you know that because of the kind of demand this type of practice enforces, the average amount of time spent on this daily is up to 90 minutes for one to become the best they can be? And this is why most won't do it. And as Colvin says this is good news! Running wholeheartedly toward things we are not good at and getting critical feedback is what most people do not want to do. And this is how the best of the best separate themselves from everyone else.

Another thing that is important about deliberate practice is that it doesn't just focus on one's physical abilities. As author Dan Millman explains in his book, *Body Mind Mastery*, "Most of us are willing to see our physical mistakes." But he continues, saying, "The path to body mind mastery also entails the willingness to acknowledge our mental and emotional foibles – to see ourselves in a less flattering light." That is so good! And this is when I see the best growth in my students. Those who embrace, not just the physical struggles, but allow the feelings to surface and acknowledge their mental states as well when they are getting broken down. Millman says, "This feeling that you are getting worse is a sign of growing awareness."

The Navy SEALs know this all too well and the importance of it to get to another level. They say when a man is beaten and defeated he is finally ready to learn. How does this help? Because when someone is defeated and truly gets in touch with their emotions they will get rid of their EGO and humble themselves to finally learn. If one really wants to get better and to the next level, they will see defeat as a great opportunity to observe their weaknesses and begin the process of growing. And the growth in one's life is priceless when they can embrace this philosophy. More enjoyment of playing one's sport is a result along with better overall performance and confidence due to the work being put in to improve. Embracing emotions and being honest with one's mistakes or weaknesses is such a great sign of courage and strength!

This is why it is so frustrating to me or I feel bad when I see others not embrace the learning process with more of an open mind. People's pride takes over and they are unwilling to get feedback or even just struggle through a drill to learn how to figure it out on their own. Remember, if we love others we will let them struggle. There is so much growth here. We may explain what we want others to do, but if they can't figure it out immediately, they need to learn how to cope with adversity and improve their problem-solving skills.

More coaches, teachers and parents need to learn this phenomenon. I'm not saying abandon students, as they should know you are there alongside them and care greatly for them, but don't spoon feed them! They may feel great in the moment if you ease them through a drill but in the long run it's the worst thing for them and opposite of what deliberate practice is. This is how they learn the discipline and emotional resiliency to not quit and keep working at it to get better. This is really beautiful to witness instead of those who just quit when the going gets tough.

To be uncommon is to have the humility to know there is never a finish line to growth. We can always get better not just physically but also emotionally, mentally, and spiritually. The earlier we learn this the more likely we are to have greater success in our entire lives because we will have the confidence to seek out challenges, stay committed to goals, and have the confidence to ask for help if needed. Deliberate practice gets the body, mind, and soul involved developing a whole person which is what we were created to be.

Deliberate Practice in the Weight Room

There is a myth that children shouldn't lift weights and I couldn't disagree with this statement more. Kids along with adults are more likely to get hurt in an uncontrolled environment like a soccer field, hockey rink, playing football or climbing trees than lifting weights with educated supervision. If people believe kids shouldn't lift weights, then kids shouldn't be carrying backpacks, groceries or doing any yard work since these are all various forms of weight lifting.

We are doing kids a disservice by keeping them out of a weight room or from training. Kids want to move and if we keep them locked up in "cages," they will go stir crazy. We need to eliminate this myth and stop stunting their growth because we think their bodies aren't ready. If this is true, then why do we see kids carry each other around or create human pyramids? Let's stop the insanity and let's get them stronger and help them grow in their confidence!

A cool fact is that the earlier kids begin training or practicing a skill, the more they will grow their brain. How amazing is that? They are making myelin in their bodies thicker. Myelin is a substance that wraps around neurons and is strengthened through repetitions and builds greater connection with the brain when they practice a skill, which is what weight lifting is – a skill. And this action happens more efficiently in kids than it does in adulthood. Those who wait until they are in high school to train will be much farther behind than those who start younger. I've seen this happen time and time again. It's disappointing because we can make up for that lost time when they could have been growing.

Author Geoff Colvin talks about a study that was done with professional pianists. He explains that the more one practiced before the age of sixteen the more myelin they had in critical parts of their brains. Training earlier in life has its advantages. Many students I have coached who begin training with us at a younger age are stronger and appear older than those who are the same age and don't train.

Another thing I have witnessed over the years is that if one begins training with a coach on deliberate practice when they are young, they show greater listening skills, they retain information better than others, and they have a greater sense of body awareness and mental toughness. Colvin talks about this as well regarding above average brains. Those who have above average brains can perceive what's going on around them, they can organize information better and they also show greater memorization skills. This is why I suggest kids train at a younger age, so they can have an advantage over their competition. But remember – it must be deliberate!

Your Body, Your Slave

Pastor, Dallas Willard teaches his students about the importance of making the body our slave. Not being a slave to the body. Uncommon champions aren't slaves to their emotions nor do they follow the desire to stay within one's comfort zone. Being uncommon means to use the body as a vehicle to push one's limits and train consistently through deliberate practice and acknowledging one's weaknesses. Become aware of the areas you need to improve on, get the mind involved in the physical activity and build greater connections with the brain to improve skills, efficiency, and connections with those around you. Leave common for those who want to stay in their comfort zone and hit the snooze button.

Let's be uncommon champions who get inspired by the greatness in others, never make excuses and make sure we are consistent with practicing deliberately knowing that is what separates us from the rest.

REFLECTION QUESTIONS

Questions for athletes:

1. What kind of practice is necessary to make it to world class and can be described as a recipe for not having fun?

2. Does deliberate practice make one mentally exhausted?

3. How long can one usually sustain deliberate practice on a daily basis?

4. Why do the Navy SEALs say it's good for one to feel defeated?

5. What does training or practicing a skill do to one's brain?

6. What does Geoff Colvin say above-average brains can do?

Questions for parents:

1. Do you believe your son or daughter is consistently doing deliberate practice?

2. How are you helping your child learn to love deliberate practice even though it is known as a recipe for not having fun?

3. How are you being an example to your child by showing them your weaknesses and being okay with making corrections?

4. Is there an area in your life that you would like to work on to keep the brain strong and growing? Is this something that you could do with your kids as a group activity?

CHAPTER 9

Principle Eight –
What is Your Legacy?

"We must learn to work for the
benefit of all humankind."
-DALAI LAMA

To Whom Much is Given…

There was a time when I was around students who were having successful careers and found that they could easily get wrapped up in all the hype and attention they were getting especially when our culture seems to idolize high-level athletes regardless of their values. During this period, I had fun going to parties on yachts, being in million-dollar homes and driving around in hundred-thousand-dollar cars. This may seem to be a great way to live life, right? So why do so many athletes lose their way, have few real values, or make poor decisions?

Kids may look at these fancy lifestyles and want to make it their goal to reach this kind of status. Unfortunately, I too was like the rest of the culture. Especially in high school where I followed the rest of the crowd and went down the wrong path: getting dressed up, going to clubs, and seeking attention from all the wrong places. I ended up making poor choices, being forced to quit competitive figure skating, had less than ideal friendships, and found myself kicked out of my home feeling like I had nowhere to turn. Scripture tells us to "Be alert and of sober mind. Your enemy the devil prowls around like a roaring lion looking for someone to devour." Luckily, I wasn't devoured. But it took years for me to begin to realize I needed to live for something different.

For years, I focused on the one thing that I felt I had left going for me: training hockey players. I was becoming more successful with coaching athletes, and my business seemed to be growing more and more. Yet, there was still something missing and I was realizing there was more to life than things of this world. There was more to life than partying on the weekends or being seen by other people that may appear to be "important" in this world.

One of my favorite pieces of scripture is, "To whom much is given, much is expected." Do you think you have been given an able body and strong mind just to be used for selfish reasons? You have been given unique abilities by God which only you can use in this life to fulfill for a purpose. What are you using your body and gifts for? To gain money, success, and status? I now know that when I was a teenager and through my young adult years I was not using the life

God gave me to make this world a better place. I was solely focused on me. I was surrounded by others who were doing the same thing. Wasting their talents away, thinking they had already made it only to come up short by making poor choices along the way.

Remember, there are two pains in life: the pain of discipline and the pain of regret. All too often I still see young adults never reach it to their goals, because they think they have already made it because they have verbal commitments to a college or they get lost along the way choosing to follow the "cool" crowd. It's so important to find mentors to guide us and remind us of what we are working for and who to honor along the way. Plus, should we only be focused on whether we just made it in hockey? What does it mean to make it in the full spectrum of life?

Did you know that our society define men and women a certain way? Boys and girls are brought up to think they should act and look based on what they see on social media, television and in the movies. Have you ever thought about how our culture defines what a real man is? What about what it means to be a woman? Unfortunately, men are brought up in this society to believe that they need to have big muscles, lots of money, a powerful status, and beautiful women at their side in order to be considered successful. There is no talk about building strong relationship with others, treating others with compassion nor how to make this world a better place. On the other side of the spectrum, women tend to believe they must be perfect, look pretty and not to be outspoken. No wonder there is so much bullying going on, isolation and anxiety.

In her book *Daring Greatly*, author Brené Brown dissects deep-rooted emotions like shame and vulnerability. These are extremely powerful emotions that can cause us to live our lives small and inauthentic because who wants to feel shame or unaccepted by others. The great news though is if we work to overcome shame and embrace vulnerability we find our life's purpose and truly transform into the creation God wants us to be. This takes a lot of courage to do but the results are joy, confidence and building a culture with more enjoyable relationships. We don't become isolated or try to be something we're not. We live more wholeheartedly.

This is why training environments need to change, coaches and teachers need to change, and the classrooms need to change. If we embrace vulnerability by knowing we are all created equal instead of trying to show off to another we can finally enjoy life a little more and become our authentic selves. There is such a better way to live life which leads to more enjoyment, trust, and love. And guess what? It can all begin by accepting others through a simple high-five. Especially when we see our friends, classmates, teammates or even strangers struggling.

As Brené Brown says, "The two most powerful forms of connection are love and belonging." Who doesn't want that for their child, their family, and the world? Therefore, we need to remember if we are not careful, we will search to find our love and belonging in things that are empty and futile. We seek out love from those who will only use us. We surround ourselves with people who only want to enjoy the success we are having or be around money and fame. Jesus warns us to not have any idols before Him. We cannot serve God and money.

This is why it is so important that when we have success through the gifts God has given us to remember where those gifts came from. It isn't from our own work alone. And if we aren't careful we will work for the approval and acceptance strictly from others which causes us to mix up where our identity comes from and pushes God out of the equation. You have to keep in mind that sports, no matter how successful one is or how long one plays for, it will always come to an end.

Motivational speaker Michael Massucci demonstrates the importance of focusing on one's legacy by using a timeline. Most kids begin playing sports around the age of eight years old. Most organized sports are finished once one graduates from high school. That's ten years of playing a sport. For those who do make it on to a college team, there will be an additional period of only four years to play. After that, if one moves on to the professional level the average career only lasts another five years. If you do the math, the average hockey player will be done playing around 25 to 30 years of age. That means if the average lifespan is currently 80 years old, there is another 50 years of life to live after hockey! So should we focus just on building athletes or should we focus on using the journey of being an athlete to become the best person we can be? We need to realize that life is much longer and deeper than a short athletic career, wouldn't you say?

The point I really want to make is, what if we got more people to teach kids there is a more purposeful life to live other than just for accolades and status in professional sports and business? Being an uncommon champion is about living for others, honoring God, and making this world a better place. Being uncommon is being a leader who understands one's platform, not so people can look up at you on stage but instead speaking to those who are listening about making a difference in the world and being that example who changes the world. Your gifts were given to you for a specific reason and if they go unused it will be like a part of God died inside of you. These gifts are so much more than how fast, strong, or powerful one can be. Those are all selfish and do nothing by themselves to make this world a better place. It's about your values and the choices you make to help those around you become better.

Everyone will have a different platform. The important thing is to realize there is a platform to use your gifts given to you by God for a purpose. It's important to treat others well through the journey, give back to society and be an example of having strong meaningful relationships. Success isn't about how big of a contract one can get. Success is how well you love others.

Every day ask yourself what is it that you are doing to not just improve you but also help those around you. People will tell you that one person can't change the world, but they can. Mother Theresa was one person, Ghandi was one person, Nelson Mandela was one person. But it does take a village. It takes a village to become all that God wants you to become which ultimately can change the world.

Don't forget to find mentors who will hold you accountable along your journey, otherwise you will get lost in the crowd and be conformed to this world instead of separating yourself from the rest. You were born to lead. You were born for a purpose. Live in a way that leaves a powerful, positive message to others. And it starts right now. Are you ready? Always ask yourself what more you can be doing for the person next to you instead of what they can do for you. Have compassion for others, be kind to everyone, and love one another. Treat others with respect, stay humble and encourage those who struggle.

When you do make it to your goals, remember to thank all those who sacrificed to help you along the way. Glorify God in all you do. Serve Him and not money. For you cannot serve them both. There is a reason scripture says, "Pride comes before the fall." Therefore, always keep working to improve because there is never a finish line. God has blessed you with a life to be here, but it's not for selfish reasons. Making the decision to leave a positive legacy will bring great joy not only in your life but to all those around. Here's to leaving common for someone else for you were born to be an uncommon champion.

REFLECTION QUESTIONS

Questions for athletes:

1. How does our culture define what being a man/woman looks like?

2. Does our culture teach us to focus on worldly success or to build values that honor God?

3. What does Brené Brown say are the two most powerful forms of connection?

4. How can we feel love and that we belong in this world without getting caught up in following the wrong crowd or wanting approval from others?

5. No matter how far one makes it in their sport, will it eventually end?

6. What does an uncommon champion look like in regard to what they are doing for the world?

Questions for parents:

1. Based on how our culture defines men and women, have you fallen into these "norms" instead of being your authentic self?

2. Where have you focused on worldly success and wanting acceptance from others rather than just from God?

3. Are you focused on your son or daughter getting to the highest level or are you focused on them learning values to become a person who changes the world for good?

4. How are you helping your son or daughter not do things to "fit in" but instead be their authentic selves?

5. Do you feel you still do things as an adult to "fit in" or find acceptance from others?

CHAPTER 10:

Obstacles to Becoming Uncommon

*"Success is 10 percent inspiration
and 90 percent perspiration."*
-THOMAS EDISON

I often ask God why I care so much. The amount of effort poured into kids to help them see their weaknesses is exhausting at times. The attention to detail to improve one's awareness can be downright frustrating. The hours of one-on-one time I have spent with kids talking about their character seem to be never ending. I do my best to not only coach skating but to help others understand where to get their identity from and who to glorify through their actions. The days and weeks to improve others' leadership skills have been countless. I can't forget to mention the hundreds I've challenged to make sure to choose one's friends wisely. And there have also been those awkward moments when I ask others to explain how they are making the world a better place.

The coaching industry across the board could be so much better. I've realized it is so much easier to just tell others how great they are. And this is what many coaches do. Then we also have on the other end of the spectrum coaches who use their authority and power in all the wrong ways. Carol Dweck reminds us that kids want praise but even though this may build a kid's confidence, remember it is only for a short amount of time. Please understand this is not helping kids become all they can be. Coaches who are too afraid to tell their students the uncomfortable truths are just setting these kids up for failure down the road when they will face adversity in life. Which we all know is inevitable. Yet, coaches need to understand to not use their clipboard or whistle to abuse or use kids either.

Transformational coaches know that their role is not about them. Coaches are able to truly help change lives if they take the time to learn from their past, understand their platform, and care about the lives they are influencing. This may even involve tough love. We have learned from the SEALs that to become our best selves we need to come to the realization that this world does not revolve around us. And the earlier we learn this, the better off we are. No matter how successful you become the world wasn't created just for you! Isn't it crazy that even King Solomon of the Bible who was the most powerful and richest man in the world at one time even came to realize this was an unfulfilling way to live life by just focusing on one's self!

It's important to teach others about choosing the hard right versus the easy wrong. Things like having the courage to be vulnerable and encourage others. To keep up on your homework and read more books instead of being on social media. It says "hard right" because if it were easy then everyone would be doing it. Plus, a hard life builds stronger character. An easy life is boring and builds soft character. Remember, building a life of integrity starts with the small things. We need to hold kids accountable and teach others to hold those around them accountable. Allowing others to believe in a false philosophy that it's okay to cut corners will eventually seep into all areas of one's life. Sports can be a huge platform to learn about discipline, responsibility, respect, courage, humility, and teamwork. Life is a team sport! If we continue to build athletes to become people who are selfish, don't understand commitment, or have zero integrity then we are setting them up for disaster. It may not be immediate, but they won't be the best person they can be. Too many people don't know their non-negotiables for coaches or relationships and put their kids in harm's way or on a path that can lead to less than ideal results. Many coaches may be able to help get kids to a higher level, but we need to be aware of whether these coaches are equipped to build uncommon champions who will help change the world for good. Changing the world for good starts with self-confidence, genuine relationships, and commitment to the betterment of others.

Western society is filled with comfort and luxuries. I often say to others, "This isn't a country club!" There's nothing wrong with country clubs but being too relaxed, not showing up on time, and staying within one's comfort zone will not improve one's performance or life. Showing up late to places or keeping others waiting is not being uncommon. Time is the most valuable thing you can give to another human being. And when one makes a commitment to a team or an event or job then they need to understand to respect others' time. You can't become the best you can be with poor habits or laziness. If you are on time, then you are late in my mind. Teachers and coaches need to have consequences for those who can't respect the time of other human beings. This is a small step in helping others understand that the world doesn't revolve around them and to remove selfish behavior. These are actions that lead to greater results and greater rewards.

We need to be aware of how our culture just continues to breed selfishness. Social media can give us the feeling we are liked by thousands or even millions of people who we don't even know. Our EGOs make us believe we are God. And our EGOs will want to follow the crowd. The crowd filled with common. It's easy to get a false sense that we are doing the right thing if we are around others who seem successful. They are making millions of dollars, coaches are praising everyone left and right and even making them stronger. But are they building the best boyfriends, girlfriends, future husbands, wives, and mothers and fathers? Remember, an athletic career only lasts so long and will eventually end. It's through this journey that we should be building those that will live a life of integrity, commitment to others and use their gifts not just to win titles but to build strong and healthy families, communities, and world.

Formula for a Better World

What if I were to tell you that I have a formula that could stop bullying, improve relationships, increase joy, and eliminate people from feeling lonely or depressed? Bold statement, right? Did you know that we currently live in a world that is at an all-time high of drug addictions, suicide rates, divorce and people feeling completely isolated? The need for approval and validation is everywhere. What if the Navy SEALs really do have the recipe and philosophy to change this world?

SEALs aren't only some of the strongest people I have met physically, but they are humble, selfless, and build some incredible relationships with their crews. This doesn't mean they still don't have struggles with their own personal relationships, which we can't judge or imagine due to the strain war puts on their family life. But what if we taught in schools, sports and in businesses the values the SEALs follow which I believe are deep within all of us to become all that we can be together?

Let's stop thinking we are better people just because we are better at a skill than someone else. Let's, instead, realize life can be more fulfilling when we work to be better than we were yesterday and do it together. Not against one another. Let's realize we can do more when we focus not on ourselves but on those next to us. What if more leaders in classrooms and boardrooms asked their students or employees the question, "Who's still working?" This prompts others who may be done with their work to go help others who may be struggling. What if at the end of each hour at school or at the end of the day we teach others to give high-fives and go tell another person what they did well today. Maybe they will even tell others what they still need to improve so this builds accountability, trust, and teamwork.

Kids should not be afraid to speak up because of the fear of getting laughed at. They shouldn't be afraid to ask questions or avoid the shame of possibly being wrong. Instead, if someone stutters or gets something incorrect, what if the kids next to them still gave them a high-five for their effort? How beautiful that would be? What if more teachers taught kids to box breathe before every test or at the start of each hour? Don't you think we would be building healthier minds, bodies, and souls of each individual along with deepening the trust between each other?

Yet, pride still seems to be the problem. When adults or teenagers act like they are too cool to do this I'll respond by saying, "If you think you know more than a Navy SEAL then I feel sorry for you." Scripture teaches us that we are all made in the image of God. Nowhere in the Bible does it say that if one has a better car, bigger bank account or bigger muscles then they must be a better person. We learned that high-fives create more oxytocin and serotonin to be pumped through our bodies making us feel trust and love between each other. Maybe we wouldn't have kids sitting alone at the lunchroom tables anymore or even a greater goal would be little to zero school shootings. This would help us get more in touch with vulnerability, connection, and ultimately create a more loving world.

If we followed the SEALs' techniques on breathing to help improve focus, creativity, and overall health we wouldn't only perform better, we would live longer. We need to remember yawning isn't impolite but instead is one of the healthiest things our bodies can do. We have a formula to create a world full of love and connection just by implementing a few high-fives, encouragement to one another, and box breathing with each other. And this isn't showing weakness. It's showing courage to show up and be seen by others and to get help from one another. Life isn't meant to be lived alone or to live with a mask on. Vulnerability with one another is power and creates an amazing culture of trust, awareness and belonging.

The world is full of common coaches who believe in only building stronger athletes. It can be confusing for parents to understand what is best for their kids when there are so many less-than-ideal philosophies out there. Too many people are sold on the philosophy that hard is bad and easy is good. It takes a strong village built with people of strong values who believe in creating an even better next generation. It may appear to be something that can't be easy, but there are no shortcuts to becoming all that God wants us to be.

To be that uncommon champion I believe it's about accountability with one another, embracing challenges together, and forging grit through feeding the courage wolf. Know that being uncommon is about looking around to see who you can encourage as you continue your journey to fulfilling all that God has planned for you. Therefore, here's to being all that we can be to glorify God and doing our part to make this world a better place one high-five and encouraging word at a time.

REFLECTION QUESTIONS

Questions for athletes:

1. Have you found a transformational coach that will focus on building all areas of a human being not just the physical aspect?

2. Do you know your non-negotiables for coaches, teachers, and others in your life?

3. What will our EGO cause us to possibly follow?

4. What is more important than building better athletes?

5. Are you a better person just because you have big muscles and are faster or more skilled than someone else?

6. How can we positively influence others to build a better culture, deeper relationships and ultimately a better world?

Questions for parents:

1. Do you believe it is helpful to find coaches for your child that only give them praise or tell them how great they think they are?

2. How are you helping your kids see the importance of seeing everyone as equals but still have that competitive spirit in them to want to be their best?

3. Who does your son or daughter have in their life besides you to help them stay disciplined, committed, and humble?

4. Do you believe that sports should strictly be about the physical realm and focused solely on winning?

5. Have you discussed with your child what they would do or what they could create to make this world a better place?

Further Reading

The Bible

Daring Greatly by Brené Brown

InsideOut Coaching by Joe Erhmann

The Way of a SEAL by Mark Divine

8 Weeks to SEALFIT: A Navy SEAL's Guide to Unconventional Training for Physical and Mental Toughness by Mark Divine

EGO is the ENEMY by Ryan Holiday

Just Breathe: Mastering Breathwork for Success in Life, Love, Business, and Beyond by Dan Brulé

Letters from Leaders: Personal Advice for Tomorrow's Leaders from the World's Most Influential People by Henry O. Dormann

Habitudes: Images that Form Leadership Habits and Attitudes by Dr. Tim Elmore

Twelve Pillars by Jim Rohn

Talent is Never Enough: Discover the Choices that will take you Beyond Your Talent by John Maxwell

Talent is Overrated: What Really Separates World-Class Performers from Everybody Else by Geoff Colvin

An Elite Journey: A Young Man's Leadership Story by Michael Massucci

Body Mind Mastery: Creating Success in Sport and Life by Dan Millman

7 Habits of Highly Effective People by Stephen Covey

How to Win Friends and Influence People by Dale Carnegie

Recommended Ted Talks and Videos

Courage of Famous Failures, https://www.youtube.com/watch? v=Ydeyl0vXdP0

The Power of Vulnerability, https://www.ted.com/talks/brene_brown_on_vulnerability

Grit: The Power of passion and perseverance, https://www.ted.com/talks/angela_lee_duckworth_grit_the_power_of_passion_and_perseverance

Jim Rohn, *Take Charge of your Life*, https://www.youtube.com/watch? v=Sk3UahYfG8Y

Acknowledgments

This book has been one heck of a journey in the making. First and foremost, I wouldn't be here without the Almighty God who continues to give me the drive, strength, and courage to keep persevering and blesses me more than I deserve. On my journey, I have gained so many life lessons along with bumps and bruises from competitive figure skating with hours of training, hundreds of competitions and going through the difficulties of the agony of defeat to the fleeting moments of the glory of victory. Skating has allowed me to create a business and live a dream of helping others become their best selves more than I ever thought was possible.

To the Morgan James Publishing team: Special thanks to David Hancock, CEO & Founder for believing in me and my message. To my Author Relations Manager, Tiffany Gibson, thanks for making the process seamless and easy. Many more thanks to everyone else, but especially Jim Howard, Bethany Marshall, and Nickcole Watkins.

To all the coaches, families, and students who have trusted me over the years to work with you and have continued to support my mission of making this world a better place I thank you. To the authors who have taken the time to write books and share their knowledge to help others become better leaders: John Maxwell, Napoleon Hill, Jim Rohn, Stephen Covey, Dale Carnegie, and Robin Sharma. To Mark Divine and all the speakers and coaches through the Unbeatable Mind Retreat and SEALFIT who continue to teach me about life and how to be our best selves I am forever grateful. You have all helped me realize we are here for a purpose which is to help others. It's not about being better than anyone else but about helping those next to you. To the Navy SEALs who have played such a pivotal role in helping me teach others about the importance of humility, accountability, and selflessness I want to give you a big HOOYAH! To my training crew at Competitive Edge Skating who I love like family, thank you for supporting me with my vision of changing the world for good by being examples of those who encourage one another and spread love with one high-five at a time.

ABOUT THE AUTHOR

With over 30 years of skating and training experience, Jennifer Matras is a highly sought-after skill development instructor and owner of Competitive Edge Skating, Inc (C.E.S.). C.E.S. is the result of Jennifer's commitment and passion to developing a company where athletes are provided everything  needed to reach their highest level of performance. C.E.S. offers innovative on-ice training, specified strength and conditioning training, mental training consultations, and nutritional counseling. As a nationally certified strength and conditioning specialist and an exercise physiologist, Jennifer understands the details and high standards it takes for an athlete to reach world class levels.

Born and raised in Redford Township, Michigan Jennifer began skating at the young age of three and a half. Jennifer trained daily at Detroit Skating Club in Bloomfield Hills, Michigan where she had a successful competitive figure skating career. Through 14 years of competitive figure skating, Jennifer accomplished regional championships along with competing nationwide.

Jennifer's coaching career began at the age of 18 in Michigan helping with the local basic skills program and power skating program but has expanded to working with athletes throughout the country. She continues to focus on semi-private lessons for hockey players from the Mini-Mite level to Professional level but also helps teams throughout their hockey season to develop them into champions.

After many years of providing on-ice instruction to hockey players, Jennifer enrolled into the Sports Medicine program at Eastern Michigan University and graduated as an exercise physiologist and nationally certified strength and conditioning specialist in June of 2005. Since then Jennifer and her staff have helped local varsity, junior varsity and AAA teams win many championship titles.

Throughout the years, Jennifer has helped her students understand the importance and the rewards that ongoing training brings. Jennifer aims to help each athlete move up the ranks by providing unique drills and exercises to work on balance, speed, coordination, agility, and overall body control. These key skills enable athletes to dominate in their game, make plays, and become more valuable to their team. Athletes who understand and are willing to put forth the effort required will be players who develop confidence, and more love for their game!

What brings Jennifer the most joy, though, is to not only spending time on the ice helping players become stronger on skates or more powerful in the weight room, but she also likes to help them grow as people. Knowing how important it is to become a better person rather than just become a good athlete, Jennifer enrolled in Moody's Theological Seminary in 2014. Through her combined experiences with figure skating, training with Navy SEALs in her adult life along with classes at Seminary, Jennifer has gained some unique life perspectives, coaching skills, and the knowledge of putting God first in one's life. Jennifer uses her platform as a coach to not just build better athletes but better people who know that success is about helping others around you and doing our part to make the world a better place.

Jennifer believes that life begins at the end of one's comfort zone. Therefore, she continues to enjoy challenging herself through training, reading, biking, and occasionally looking for adrenaline rush with skydiving, rollercoasters or bungee jumping. She also enjoys spending time with friends, family and her dog Roman's Chapter 12 (named after Jennifer's favorite chapter out of the Bible.)

Website: www.ceskating.com
Email: icejen9@gmail.com
Facebook: https://www.facebook.com/competitiveedgeskating/
Instagram: @Competitive_edge_skating

CPSIA information can be obtained
at www.ICGtesting.com
Printed in the USA
BVHW031510271019
562180BV00001B/54/P

9 781642 793543